A HISTORY
OF WOMEN ARTISTS

BY HUGO MUNSTERBERG

A HISTORY OF
WOMEN
ARTISTS

BY HUGO MUNSTERBERG

Clarkson N. Potter, Inc./Publisher NEW YORK

DISTRIBUTED BY CROWN PUBLISHERS, INC.

Printed in the United States of America
Published simultaneously in Canada by General Publishing
Company Limited

Inquiries should be addressed to Clarkson N. Potter,
Inc., One Park Avenue, New York, N.Y. 10016.

Designed by Shari de Miskey

Library of Congress Cataloging in Publication Data

Munsterberg, Hugo, 1916–
    A history of women artists.

    Bibliography: p.
    Includes index.
    1. Women artists—History. I. Title.
N8354.M86 1975   709'.2'2   75-19043
ISBN 0-517-52380-9

Second printing, March, 1977

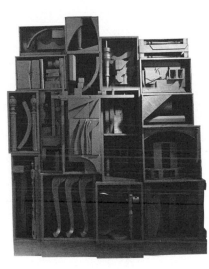

For Louise Nevelson,
who has proved that
it is indeed in their
stars, not in their
sex, that the destiny
of female artists lies

CONTENTS

PREFACE

THIS BOOK attempts to tell the story of women artists and their contribution to world art. The author has tried to relate the facts in an objective manner, avoiding as far as possible both the strident voices of the ardent feminists and the condescension and benign neglect of their male counterparts. Although it would seem that such a study is a uniquely contemporary enterprise, there is already a considerable literature on the subject, beginning with the German scholar Ernst Guhl's *Frauen in der Kunstgeschichte,* which was published in 1858. One year later came Mrs. Elizabeth Ellet's book, *Women Artists in All Ages and Countries,* and in 1876 Ellen Clayton published her *English Female Artists* in two scholarly volumes. These pioneering works were followed by J. E. Wessely's *Kunstübende Frauen* of 1884, M. Varchon's *La Femme dans l'art* of 1893, Clara Clement's *Women in the Fine Arts* of 1904, and Walter Sparrow's *Women Painters of the World,* published in 1905. By the turn of the century, the pioneer feminists of the 1800s had already made a significant contribution to the study of the female role in the arts. It is to all these early writers and to the many others who wrote monographs or biographical studies of individual women artists that the author here expresses his gratitude and indebtedness.

It would be impossible to list the many people who through their encouragement, help, and criticism have aided in this project. As so often, my wife served as both inspiration and editor. In fact, it was she, a novelist and poet, who first made me aware of the problem, and my daughter who first pointed out to me what an important role women have played in the history of photography. In addition, my research assistant, Ms. Barbara Krasnow, brought much interesting new material to my attention. I thank all of them.

I would also like to thank all the artists, collectors, museums, and galleries who so generously made available to me photographs of works in their collections. I mention particularly the staffs of the Fogg Museum and Peabody Museum of Harvard University, the Photography Department of the Metropolitan Museum of Art, the curators of the Whitney Museum and the Museum of the American Indian and, above all, Miss Betsy Burne Jones of the Smith College Museum, Miss Diana Edkins of the Museum of Modern Art, Mrs. Jain Kelly of the Witkin Gallery, and Miss Virginia Field of the Asia House Gallery, who kindly had a color transparency of a work in her possession made especially for this publication.

New Paltz, New York

Mary Benson of Pomo tribe making a basket. *Photograph courtesy of Museum of the American Indian, New York*

I WOMEN ARTISTS IN PREHISTORIC TIMES AND PRIMITIVE CIVILIZATIONS

NO ONE knows when the first female artists emerged, but there can be little doubt that the history of women's art is very ancient, probably spanning a period of some ten thousand years. Historians tend to believe that in the Old Stone Age women were not yet active in the arts. During this period men dominated society because they were the hunters who provided the food, and the magnificent cave paintings and small sculptures of the Paleolithic period are believed to have been created by male artists. That this was the case is borne out by the culture of the most primitive living people, the aboriginals of Australia, whose elaborate paintings and simple carvings are all produced by men.

With the coming of the Neolithic period, whose beginnings go back to the seventh millennium B.C., the situation changed drastically and women began to play a far more important role in cultural life. While the men hunted and raised cattle, the women worked in the fields and took care of the homes. It was under their aegis that domestic arts like weaving, straw plaiting, and pottery were developed, and it seems likely that most of these crafts were actually produced by female artists. There are a variety of reasons for this assumption, some purely archaeological, others connected with linguistic and mythological evidence, and still others based on the comparative study of contemporary societies existing on a Neolithic level of civilization. The most persuasive evidence for believing that the pottery was made by female artists is that much of it was found at domestic sites where women would have been active and that most of the wares were made for utilitarian purposes connected with the home, which was the sphere of the female members of the society. Linguistic studies of words used for the crafts in Indo-Germanic languages indicate that they were largely female terms, suggesting that these arts were closely connected with women's work. Another point is that in virtually all mythologies the invention of spinning and weaving is credited to female genius. Even in Classical Greece the deity of handicrafts was the goddess Athena, who was the particular patron of potters and weavers. The Czech scholar Joseph Poulik summarizes the situation when he says, "This cult of the Great Mother Earth, the cult of fertility, is well attested among the farming communities of the Eastern Mediterranean. The finds show, too, that woman played a very important part in such communities and was the chief factor in production. She kept the hut, worked up skins, made the pottery, sowed, reaped and milled the grain, made bread, etc."[1]

While practically nothing of the textile work, matting, and basketry of the Neolithic period has survived, a great many Neolithic ceramic wares have been discovered. Although the earliest of these works were no doubt purely utilitarian, a rich repertoire of ceramic shapes and decorative designs was soon developed. The forms of these vessels were usually strong and simple, with sturdy, swelling bodies that were made by hand without the help of the potter's wheel. The decorative designs with which they are often covered were usually painted or incised on the surface of the vessel, although occasionally they were appliquéd or molded. As a rule, the ornaments are geometric in character with all kinds of spirals, chevrons, zigzags, lozenges, checkers, and similar patterns.

The earliest of these wares, which date from about 6500 B.C., were found in Anatolia and Iran, but this type of ornamented Neolithic pottery, much of it of great beauty, can be found in many parts of the world from Japan and China in the Far East to the Danube region and the Balkans in the West, Thailand and India in the South, and Turkestan and Scandinavia in the North. Especially fine are the magnificent painted beakers from Susa in western Iran dating from the fourth millennium B.C. and the molded and rope-impressed Jōmon vessels from third millennium Japan, many of them no doubt the work of women potters. They show what great artistic gifts women possessed, for in these works female artists produced masterpieces of ceramics, equaling if not surpassing the finest pottery made by later, more sophisticated, civilizations.

A similar situation exists in the primitive tribal societies of modern times. In present-day Africa, crafts are largely the work of women whereas sculpture, which is considered the more significant art form because it deals with magic and the sacred, is always the work of men. The only exceptions are the clay sculptures, which, being made of pottery, are considered women's work. Outstanding among these are the Mbari sculptures of the Ibo people of Nigeria, the sculptural pots of the Mangbetu of Zaire, the grave figures of the Agni women of Ghana, and the clay dolls of the Bamessing and the Bamesi of the Cameroon grassland. Occasionally, specific groups of women potters are given the right to produce clay grave sculptures, as is the case among the Dakakari of northeast Nigeria, who make images of elephants and other wild animals, equestrian statues, and human figures. However, this is very much the exception. The great bulk of ceramics are purely utilitarian and serve the practical needs of the community. In some villages, virtually all the women participate in the ceramic production. Usually the

[1] J. Poulik, *Prehistoric Art* (London: Spring Books, 1956), p. 20.

Neolithic pot from Czechoslovakia, circa 5000 B.C.
Brno Museum

Neolithic jar from Japan, circa 4000 B.C. *Collection of William Wolff, New York*

Modern African bottle of Mangbetu tribe, 19th or 20th century. *Private collection, New York*

output is intended primarily for personal use, but the surplus may be sold in the market or exchanged.

African women, in addition to making pottery, often create textiles of all kinds and basketry, mats, and beadwork. However, these crafts are not necessarily restricted to women. The custom may differ from tribe to tribe, or even village to village, and is usually dictated by tradition rather than by the artistic gifts or interests of the individual. Among the Dogon people of Mali, who are perhaps the most traditional of today's African tribes, the women make the pottery, spin the cotton fiber, and dye the cloth, and the men do the more strenuous tasks of wood carving as well as weaving and basketmaking. On the other hand, among the Yoruba people of Ede in Nigeria, not only pottery but all weaving and dyeing are done by women. A rare exception is the Hausa people of northern Nigeria, where the pottery is made by men. However, as Louise Jefferson points out, "There is usually a sharp dividing line between the crafts practiced by men and those practiced by women with the men in most regions responsible for house-building, tool making, and carving, while the women are adept at dyeing, spinning, making pottery and weaving."[2] Most books on African art deal mainly with the sculptures, which are indeed among the great carvings in world art. But the African textiles should not be neglected, for the finest of the weavings of Nigeria and the tie-dyed cloth from West Africa are often very beautiful in design and color, showing what remarkable work African women can produce when they are given an opportunity to express themselves in the visual arts.

And so it is in other primitive civilizations of the modern world: as in Africa, the various fields of artistic activity are divided up between the sexes; the men create the sculpture and the painting and the crafts are relegated to the women. In Oceania, sculpture, considered the most important art since it was connected with the cult of the spirits, is entirely the province of male artists while the women produce pottery and, above all, tapa cloth decorated with abstract designs made by painting or stenciling. Women also make baskets and mats as well as the featherwork so characteristic of this area. The situation is similar among the Eskimo, where it is the men who make the sculptures and masks and the women who produce the garments and the decorative leatherwork.

That sex governed both the choice of the medium and the importance of the art is most clearly demonstrated by the North American Indians. While the male-dominated, aggressive, warlike societies of the Northwest Coast Indians excelled in wooden sculpture like the magnificent totem poles, the female-dominated Pueblo culture of the Southwest, which was gentle and peace loving, produced largely decorative arts, with their pottery and basketry achieving rare excellence and playing the dominant role in their artistic culture. In each society the other art form—crafts in one and sculpture in the other—played a strictly subordinate role because it was not considered primary for the purposes of the society, nor was it congenial to the dominant sexual group. However, in some Indian societies these roles varied. For example, among the Hopi, the men did the weaving, whereas in contemporary Middle America both men and women worked in clay. In the case of the Plains Indians, the painted designs on animal skins were executed by men if they were realistic and by women if they were geometric.

As Frederick Dockstader says:

[2] L. Jefferson, *The Decorative Arts of Africa* (New York: Viking Press, 1973), p. 16.

Basket by Datsolalee of Washo tribe, 20th century. *Museum of the American Indian, New York*

It is interesting to note the degree to which we judge the whole culture of a tribe by the work of its women folk. For much of the material culture of the American Indian is the product of feminine activity. True, the Hopi men wove, Plains men painted their ceremonial objects, and Iroquois men carved wooden utensils and masks; but I think it is far more significant that we tend to base much of our evaluation of the aboriginal culture of the Indian on pottery, basketry, bead work, costuming, and so on—most of which was done by women.[3]

This is particularly true among the Southwestern Indian cultures where the pottery of the Pueblo women and the rugmaking of the Navaho women were the dominant art forms. It is thought that 90 percent of the Pueblo women were potters and that this tradition was a very ancient one dating from prehistoric times. Interestingly enough, however, archaeological data from the Papago Pueblo suggest that men were permitted to help the women potters by fetching clay and carving the wooden paddles. In modern times, men often help in the firing or decoration of the pots, but they are not really essential to the production.

That this tradition still survives is apparent in the work of Maria Martinez, the most celebrated of all modern American Indian artists. Her fame and success far surpass those of any Indian male artist, including contemporary Indian painters. Basing her work on traditional Indian wares discovered by modern archaeologists, she has evolved a style distinctly her own but at the same time truly Indian, using the same shapes and techniques that her ancestors at the San Ildefonso Pueblo had employed centuries ago. Equally accomplished are the contemporary Navaho women who produce the finest rugs and blankets in North America, showing a beauty of pattern and color and a variety and individuality of design unique among Indian crafts. The same is true among the Indians of the Northwest, whose women produced the magnificent woven blankets and baskets and whose men worked largely in wood.

A much older Indian textile tradition existed in ancient Peru. In the valleys of the

---

[3]F. J. Dockstader, *Indian Art in Middle America* (Greenwich, Connecticut: New York Graphic Society, 1964), p. 22.

Indian pottery vessel from Zia Pueblo, 19th century. *Peabody Museum, Harvard University*

Pottery jar by Maria Martinez of San Ildefonso Pueblo, 20th century. *Museum of the American Indian, New York*

northern part of the country, beautifully designed textiles have been found dating from as early as 2500 B.C. This tradition continued for many centuries, culminating in the magnificent woven and embroidered mummy wrappings found at the cemeteries of Paracas and Nazca in southern Peru and dating from the centuries just before and after the time of Christ. Exhibiting beautiful designs and gorgeous color patterns, these textiles are among the finest ever made. They served a great variety of purposes. Clothing was considered of supreme importance, especially among the Incas, whose garments were made by the fairest and most talented young women of the realm. The textiles were also used as wall hangings, samplers, quilts, sacks, slings, and, above all, for grave and sacrificial offerings. Neither sculpture nor painting occupied as important a place as textiles in the culture of the ancient Indians of Peru.

Navajo blanket, 19th century. *Emmerich Gallery, New York*

Wool blanket of Tlingit tribe, 19th century. *Peabody Museum, Harvard University*

Baskets from Tlingit tribe, 19th century.
Peabody Museum, Harvard University

Indian woman of Campas tribe in Peru weaving. *Photograph courtesy Museum of the American Indian, New York*

A HISTORY OF WOMEN ARTISTS

Feather mantle, Peruvian, circa A.D. 1200. *Nelson Gallery, Kansas City, Missouri*

According to all accounts, this art was almost wholly the product of women, who are said to have worked much of the day making textiles of wool and cotton. They spun even while walking, and workbaskets found in Peruvian graves always contain spindles, balls of cotton and wool yarn or thread, and other weaving materials. However, weaving was by no means restricted to common people nor did it serve only utilitarian needs. This art, especially among the Incas, had a central role in the entire life of the society. Professor Bushnell says:

> Those who served the Emperor included specially skilled weavers, who made fine clothing for him. It is difficult to exaggerate the importance of cloth in the Inca polity, and examples like the textiles found in Paracas mummies suggest strongly that this was nothing new, in fact the general excellence of Peruvian weaving would make it surprising if it were otherwise. In Inca times the weavers had to make cloth for the ruler and the gods from materials provided by the State, and in return the State gave them the materials from which to weave their own clothes. The finest fabrics were reserved for the ruler, and gifts of them from him were highly appreciated. Cloth was used in all sorts of gift exchanges, in the crises of life, and for sacrifice. It was second only to food in the army's rations, and enormous quantities were found by the Spaniards in the storehouses, in addition to those which were burnt to keep them out of their [the Spaniards'] hands.[4]

As a result of the great importance attached to textiles, this art far excelled the sculpture, painting, and architecture of the ancient Peruvians. It also represents a high point in the history of textiles, and it is one of the greatest achievements of female creativity in the art of the world.

[4]G. H. Bushnell, *Peru* (London, 1956), p. 134.

2 WOMEN ARTISTS OF ANTIQUITY AND THE MIDDLE AGES

WITH THE establishment of the great historic civilizations of Egypt and Mesopotamia, the importance of women in the arts declined. The great temples and palaces built by the Sumerians, the Egyptians, the Assyrians, and the Persians were wholly the work of men, as were the large stone sculptures and wall paintings. Women tended to be limited to their family and home so that they had little opportunity to receive any kind of artistic training. The sole exceptions were probably spinning and weaving. In Egypt, the goddess Neith was credited with the invention of weaving, and among the Sumerians of ancient Mesopotamia, Uttu was the goddess of weaving, an art referred to in a Sumerian text as "that which goes with womanhood." It was still looked upon as a female occupation, and no doubt many of the beautiful fabrics produced both for personal adornment and for hangings and decoration were the work of female artists.

Little is known about the role of women in the artistic life of Greece and Rome. Our only source of information is the Roman author Pliny who, in the early years of the first Christian century, said:

Women, too, have been painters: Timarete, the daughter of Mikon, painted an Artemis at Ephesos in a picture of a very archaic style. Eirene, the daughter and pupil of the painter Kratinos, painted a maiden at Eleusis, Kalypso painted portraits of an old man, of the juggler Theodoros, and of the dancer Alkisthenes; Aristarete, the daughter and pupil of Nearchos, painted an Asklepios. Iaia of Kyzikos, who remained single all her life, worked at Rome in the youth of Marcus Varro, both with the brush and with the

Detail of Alexander mosaic, from House of Faun, Pompeii, based on 4th century B.C. painting.
National Museum, Naples

cestrum on ivory. She painted chiefly portraits of women, and also a large picture of an old woman at Naples, and a portrait of herself, executed with the help of a mirror. No artist worked more rapidly than she did, and her pictures had such merit that they sold for higher prices than those of Sopolis and Dionysios, well-known contemporary painters, whose works fill our galleries. Olympias also was a painter; of her we know only that Autoboulos was her pupil.[5]

Unfortunately, none of the works of these women painters has survived. It may be assumed, however, that their style and subjects did not differ materially from those of the male artists of the time. The emergence of female artists is believed to have been largely a development of the Hellenistic period when women were permitted to take a more active part in the cultural life of the Greeks. Among the female artists mentioned during this period was Kallo, whose pictures presented to the temple of Venus were favorably commented upon by a classical poetess, while the artist herself, whose name means beautiful, was praised for being as lovely as her work. But the most famous woman artist was Helena, who is said to have painted a battle scene showing Alexander vanquishing Darius, a picture on which the celebrated mosaic in Pompeii is believed to be based. The fact that all these women were painters rather than sculptors or

[5]Quoted from *The Elder Pliny's Chapters on the History of Art,* translated by K. Jex-Blake (Chicago: University of Chicago Press, 1968), p. 171.

architects suggests that there was little resistance to women working in this field. The only woman sculptor who is mentioned in Greek literature is Kora, the daughter of the potter Dibutades, who is said to have lived in the Greek city of Corinth during the middle of the seventh century B.C. It is to her that the invention of relief sculpture is attributed. While it may well be true that this young woman might have assisted her father in his work, it seems unlikely that at such an early date she was an important artist in her own right. And, of course, relief sculpture had been used in Greece for centuries, having been invented several thousand years earlier.

In Rome, where women were kept at home, female artists played a less important role. Several Roman writers speak of spinning and weaving as the only artistic activities suitable for women, and there is little evidence that women artists were given any opportunity to develop their gifts. The one painter specifically mentioned is of Greek origin. However, since there is a painting excavated at Herculaneum and now in the Naples Museum that shows a woman painting a picture, there must have been at least a few women artists doing easel paintings. The idea that a woman's place was in the home was carried over to early Christian times. Clement of Alexandria put it very bluntly when he said that the wife is to "exercise herself in spinning and weaving, and superintending the cookery if necessary." Under such circumstances, it is not surprising that the female contribution to the arts declined.

Compared to antiquity, the Middle Ages offered far greater opportunities. Queens, princesses, and noble ladies exerted considerable power and influence, and they were often left in control of large estates during the absence of their lords. However, from an artistic point of view, the nuns were even more important, especially the abbesses, for the nunneries like the monasteries were great centers of cultural activity during this entire period. Not only are we told in numerous chronicles and church records of female patrons of the arts but also of both secular and religious women artists who made a remarkable contribution to the arts of their time. Étienne Borleau in his *Livre des Métiers,* among the five hundred crafts he mentions, lists at least five as the exclusive province of women, and he says that in many other fields women worked along with men. The areas in which they particularly excelled were embroidery, weaving, and miniature painting, as well as copying and illuminating sacred books.

A number of medieval miniatures are actually signed by women or traditionally attributed to them, and one of these artists, the nun Guda, even included her self-portrait in a homily she illustrated, which is now in the collection of the municipal library in Frankfort on the Main. Another famous manuscript that bears a woman's signature is the Beatus Apocalypse of 970, now in the Gerona Cathedral, on which the name of the nun Ende appears along with that of a monk; while in Italy, Donella, a female illuminator, is mentioned in the 1271 memorial of Bologna. The greatest and most remarkable of these women are Saint Hildegard of Bingen and the nun Herrade of Landesberg. Hildegard was a mystic whose writings (now in the state library in Wiesbaden) show a deep spiritual insight that is reflected in the miniatures illustrating her visions. Herrade, who called herself a bee who gathered honey from all kinds of flowers, was responsible for the *Hortus deliciarum,* a kind of medieval encyclopedia and book of instructions for the nuns under her care. Written around 1200, it was a masterpiece of medieval illumination. Unfortunately, it was destroyed in a fire in 1870.

While German religious establishments were outstanding for their female illuminators, England was the leading country for all kinds of textiles. English embroideries, tapestries, and weaving enjoyed great fame and are found not only in the

A HISTORY OF WOMEN ARTISTS

Evangelist Saint Mark, from Gospel of the Abbess Uta. *Collection of Bavarian State Library, Munich*

The Four Evangelists, from Beatus manuscript by the nun Ende. *Gerona Cathedral*

Ornamental animals and writing from Beatus manuscript by the nun Ende. *Gerona Cathedral*

A HISTORY OF WOMEN ARTISTS

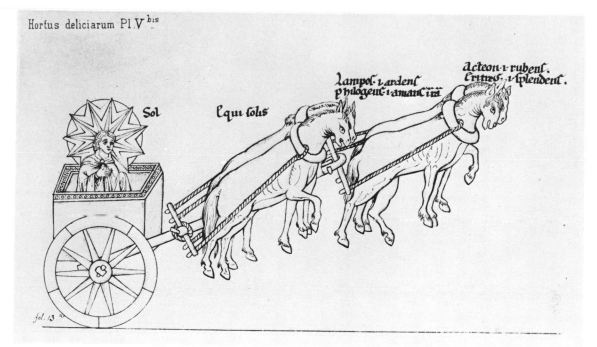

Miniature painting of sun, from the *Hortus deliciarum,* by Herrade of Landesberg, formerly in Strassburg Library

Miniature painting of Lamentation, from the *Hortus deliciarum,* by Herrade of Landesberg, formerly in Strassburg Library

German embroidery by Sophia, Hedwigis, and Lucardis, 14th century. *Metropolitan Museum of Art, New York*

churches and palaces of Great Britain but on the Continent as well. Nunneries were the centers for this work, but groups of secular female artists were also active, with the greatest period extending from the tenth to the fourteenth century. By the end of the Middle Ages, guilds of male craftsmen became very active, relegating the nuns to a more marginal position. A great many medieval textiles of all kinds have survived, often carefully preserved by the very church for which they were originally made. They show considerable variety not only in technique and design but also in their function, serving as hangings, curtains, banners, altar covers, tapestries, carpets, religious vestments, and other garments.

The most celebrated of all these works is the eleventh-century Bayeux Tapestry, really a large and very long embroidery in wool on linen, depicting the story of William's conquest of England in a very vivid and detailed manner. It is traditionally ascribed to Queen Matilda and her ladies, but modern scholars tend to question this attribution. Even earlier are the stole and maniple of Saint Cuthbert, which are in Durham Cathedral and were embroidered by Queen Aelfled around 900. Another tenth-century embroidery is the curtain made in 991 by the widow of Brihtnoth, ealdorman of the East Saxons, which shows the principal episodes of her husband's life. Germany, Switzerland, and France also produced remarkable textile work during this period. Of the German examples, the most famous is the woven tapestry in the Convent in Quedlinburg, which dates from the thirteenth century and is attributed to Saint Agnes of Meissen. Interestingly enough, it represents a classical subject, the "Marriage of Mercury with Philosophy." Of particular importance is the detail in the Passion Carpet in Bamberg showing two nuns working at the loom, a scene that provides visual evidence for the prominent role women played in textile manufacture.

Battle of Hastings and Embarkation of William, from the Bayeux Tapestry, Norman, 11th century. *Collection of Bayeux Tour Hall, Bayeux, France*

3 WOMEN ARTISTS OF THE RENAISSANCE AND BAROQUE PERIODS

IN ITS immediate effect, the end of the medieval period brought a decline in the position of women and undermined the role that they had played in the arts. The cult of Mary and the ideal of Courtly Love were no longer so dominant. The nunneries, which had been such active artistic and cultural centers, ceased to be of great importance, while textiles became more and more the province of male professionals organized into guilds to which women had no access. In fact, the fifteenth century saw little important artistic activity on the part of any women. Walter Sparrow in his *Women Painters of the World*[6] reproduces the work of a few Italian religious painters, most of them nuns belonging to the school of Siena, the most conservative of Italian painting, but none of them are artists of any distinction. There is also a tradition that Jan van Eyck's sister Margaret was a miniature painter who worked for the Burgundian court. The sixteenth-century art historian Karel van Mander, "the Netherlandish Vasari," calls her a gifted Minerva and tells us that she lived her days in single blessedness. Although several pictures have been attributed to Margaret, the earliest mention of her dates from 1565, well over one hundred years after her death, and modern scholars tend to doubt her having been an artist.

In the long run, the liberating and creative forces of the Renaissance proved to be very fruitful for women's art. The ideal Renaissance woman is perhaps best described

[6]W. S. Sparrow, *Women Painters of the World* (London and New York, 1905), plates 34–35.

by Baldassare Castiglione in his famous book of 1518, *The Courtier*, in which he has Guiliano de Medici discourse on the *donna di palazzo*. According to him, the court lady should preserve her femininity and, at the same time, display a knowledge of letters and arts, and be able to entertain at court. In short, instead of presiding over her household and leaving home only to go to church, which had been the ideal role during the medieval period, the Renaissance woman was supposed to become part of the world and acquire the cultural accomplishments suitable to the spirit of the age. As a result, female artists of much greater individuality began to emerge during the sixteenth century.

Among the women painters of the Renaissance, the most famous was Sofonisba Anguissola, whom Vasari refers to in his *Lives of the Painters, Sculptors and Architects*, where he mentions having seen several of her portraits which were so lifelike and vivid that they "lacked speech only." He goes on to say that she had been called to Spain to paint the portrait of the queen, which she sent to Rome with the following letter:

Holy Father, I have learned from your Nuncio that you desired a portrait of my royal mistress by my hand. I considered it a singular favor to be allowed to serve your Holiness, and I asked Her Majesty's permission, which was readily granted, seeing the paternal affection which your Holiness displays to her. I have taken this opportunity of sending it by this knight. It will be a great pleasure to me if I have gratified your Holiness' wish, but I must add that, if the brush could represent the beauties of the queen's soul to your eyes, they would be marvelous. However, I have used the utmost diligence to present what art can show, to tell your Holiness the truth. And so I humbly kiss your most holy feet.

Madrid, September 16, 1561
Your Holiness' most humble servant
Sofonisba Anguissola[7]

According to Vasari, the Pope was delighted with the portrait and sent in return gifts worthy of Sofonisba's talent. He replied:

Pius Papa IV Dilecta In Christo Filia. We have received the portrait of our dear daughter the Queen of Spain, which you have sent. It has given us the utmost satisfaction both for the person represented, whom we love like a father for the piety and the good qualities of her mind, and because it is well and diligently executed by your hand. We thank you and assure you that we shall treasure it among our choicest possessions, and commend your marvelous talent which is the least among your numerous qualities. And so we send you our benediction. May God save you. Dat. Roma die 15 Octobris 1561.[8]

Born in Cremona, Sofonisba was one of six daughters of a North Italian nobleman, all of whom became painters. The date of her birth is not known. It was once believed that she was born in 1528, but recent scholarship tends toward a later date, possibly between 1535 and 1540. She was a student first of Bernardino Campi and later of Bernardino Gatti. In addition to being a painter, she was also an accomplished musician and a scholar, in keeping with the new ideal of the cultured woman. Michelangelo

[7]G. Vasari, *The Lives of the Painters, Sculptors and Architects,* trans. A. B. Hinds (London, 1927), vol. 3, pp. 319–20.
[8]Ibid., pp. 319–20.

himself praised her work, and Van Dyck, who visited her in 1623 when she was old and blind, reported that she was still the center of a lively circle and that he learned more from her during this one meeting than from any other source. Her artistic career was a triumph, starting with her early success in Italy and followed by a twenty-year sojourn in Spain. Arriving in Madrid in 1559, Sofonisba was welcomed with great honors by King Philip II, who was an enthusiastic patron of the arts. She was placed among the ladies-in-waiting at the royal court and received a handsome stipend as a court painter. While in Spain, she executed numerous portraits of the king, queen, princes, and princesses, some of which are still extant. After marrying a Sicilian nobleman, she settled down in Palermo, but, after the death of her husband, moved to Genoa where she married for a second time. Her later years were troubled by blindness, but she continued to be intellectualiy alert and active in cultural matters. She died in 1625.

Opinions about Sofonisba Anguissola's achievement have differed widely. Most of her contemporaries admired her talent and praised her work, no doubt partly influenced by the fact that she was the first woman artist to achieve such great fame. Although she was an accomplished painter, certainly the equal of most of her contemporaries, her work is neither original nor distinguished. Had she been a man, she would probably be unknown today or at best considered one of the minor members of the North Italian school of painting of the second half of the sixteenth century. About fifty of her works survive today, scattered over many public and private collections. Most of them are portraits, and there is no doubt that it was primarily in this genre that she made her most important contribution. Her work was clearly influenced by the school of Venice, which was dominant in northern Italy at this time, but she also reflects, especially in her mature work, the influence of the Mannerists, notably Bronzino, who was the most outstanding and elegant portrait painter of that school. A certain aloofness and calm dignity in which she approached her sitters, as well as the shallow space she used, both point in this direction.

Two well-known Italian women painters of the sixteenth century were Lavinia Fontana and Marietta Robusti, both of them, as with so many female artists, the daughters of painters. Marietta Robusti's father was Tintoretto, and she is said to have assisted him along with her brothers Domenico and Marco. It is believed that she was born in 1560 and died at the age of thirty in 1590. Tradition has it that she was a great favorite of her father's and that she developed into a distinguished portrait painter in her own right, but no work has survived that can be attributed to her with absolute certainty. Several pictures that have been assigned to her, such as a portrait of a seated old man with a boy in Vienna, suggest that she worked in a style very close to that of her father, probably forming part of his workshop.

In contrast to Marietta Robusti, Lavinia Fontana far surpassed her father Prospero, who was a minor painter of the school of Bologna where she was born in 1552. She studied with her father along with Ludovico Carracci, who became one of the most famous masters of sixteenth-century Italian painting. Lavinia married a fellow painter, Gian Paolo Zappi, and had three children. Interestingly enough, her husband gave up his career to care for their family and to help his wife paint the garments of the figures and the frames of her pictures. She was enormously successful, especially with her portraits, and her works were much admired for the beauty of their color and the detail of the clothes and the jewelry. She was also outstanding as a religious painter, and some of her most famous works are large altarpieces executed for the churches of Bologna and later of Rome, where she went in 1600. Popes Gregory XIII—who came from her

Portrait of a Boy, by Sofonisba Anguissola, 16th century. *Walters Art Gallery, Baltimore*

Portrait of a Lady with a Lap Dog, by Lavinia Fontana, 16th century. *Walters Art Gallery, Baltimore*

native city—Clement VIII, and Paul V were patrons of hers, and the Roman aristocracy took her up with great enthusiasm. In fact, she became one of the most popular portrait painters of her day. Popes, cardinals, ambassadors, and the nobility sat for her, and it is said that she earned more for her work than Van Dyck. A self-portrait shows her as an art collector and connoisseur of antiquity, indicating that she was a woman of culture as well as a practicing artist. Her largest work was a more than life-size rendering of the stoning of Saint Stephen, which she undertook as an altarpiece for the church of Saint Paul's outside the Walls, in Rome, and which was destroyed in the fire of 1823. Of her surviving works, the most ambitious is the *Visit of the Queen of Sheba,* now in the National Gallery in Dublin. Some miniature portraits of artists, among them Tintoretto, Parmigianino, Carracci, and Barocci, are also attributed to her. The esteem in which she was held was so great that she was elected a member of the Roman Academy, a rare honor for a woman artist, and it is said that when she passed near the seat of the Lord of Sora and Vignola, he himself, accompanied by his retainers, came out to meet her, an honor usually bestowed only on royal personages. Philip II of Spain paid her a thousand ducats for her work, and others gave her splendid gifts in exchange for her paintings. Certainly no other female artist had ever enjoyed such success and, when she died in Rome in 1614, her death was widely mourned.

While Italy led the way in recognizing women artists and awarding them a position of respect and honor, there were similar tendencies in the north. The German artist Albrecht Dürer, visiting the Netherlands in 1521, was so impressed by the work of the eighteen-year-old Susanne Horenbout, daughter of the painter Gehrart Horenbout, that he gave her a florin for a drawing of Christ and marveled that a female could create such excellent work. Born in Ghent in 1503, she became a celebrated miniaturist and was invited to England by Henry VIII where she pursued a successful career and died in Worcester in 1545. Another well-known woman painter of the northern school was Catharina van Hemessen, who was active in Antwerp around the middle of the sixteenth century. Almost nothing is known about her life, not even the dates of her birth and death. She too was the daughter of an artist and enjoyed considerable fame. In fact, when Queen Mary of Hungary abdicated in the Netherlands and returned to Spain, she took Catharina and her husband and employed her at the royal court. Relatively few works can be definitely attributed to her. The most striking is a self-portrait of 1548 which shows her at the easel, indicating how seriously she took her position as an artist. Another fine example is a male portrait of 1552, now in the National Gallery in London, which suggests that she was a very elegant portrait painter, working in a style similar to that of François Clouet and Hans Holbein.

During the Baroque period, women painters became both more numerous and more prominent. Not only in Italy and Flanders but also in Holland, France, Germany, Spain, and England, women artists began to play an important role. According to Luigi Crespi's 1769 book about the lives of Bolognese painters, during the sixteenth and seventeenth centuries twenty-three women painters were active in Bologna alone, and there were many others in Rome, Florence, Naples, Genoa, and other Italian cities. Women painters were still very rare in the fifteenth century and none of them developed distinctive artistic styles. In the sixteenth century, they were much admired because they were still so exceptional, but by the seventeenth century they were beginning to take their rightful place alongside their male colleagues.

By far the most remarkable was the Italian painter Artemisia Lomi, known as Artemisia Gentileschi. Born in Rome in 1593, she received her early training under her

Portrait of Nobleman, by Catharina van Hemessen, 16th century. *Reproduced by courtesy of the Trustees, The National Gallery, London*

father Orazio Gentileschi, a painter of the Caravaggio school, and Agostino Tassi. A brilliant and precocious girl, she showed remarkable promise and entered the Accadèmia del Disegno in Florence in 1616. She returned to Rome in 1624 but the artistic climate, which tended toward Classicism, was not congenial to her Caravaggesque taste, and she went to Naples in 1630, where she remained for the rest of her life with the exception of a brief period in England when she visited her father during 1638 and 1639. She died around 1652, but the exact date has not yet been established.

Next to Caravaggio himself, who died in 1610, Artemisia Gentileschi was the finest Caravaggesque painter in Italy and one of the greatest painters of her period. The two outstanding women artists of the sixteenth century, Sofonisba Anguissola and Lavinia Fontana, cannot be compared to the best male artists of their time, but Artemisia can hold her own with the finest of her male contemporaries and, interestingly enough,

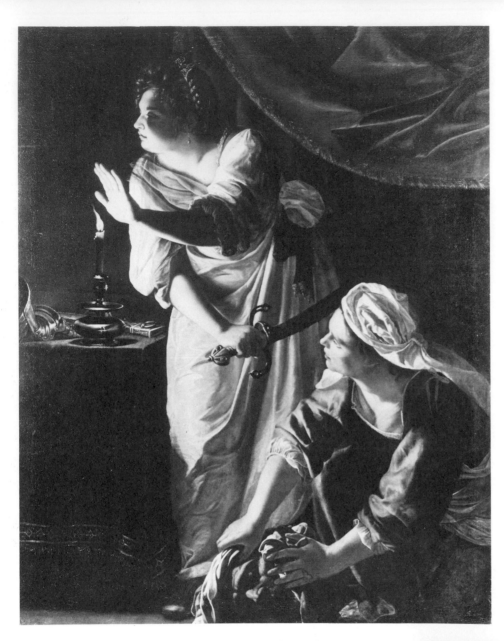

Judith and Maidservant with the Head of Holofernes, by Artemisia
Gentileschi, 17th century. *Detroit Institute of Arts*

Judith Cutting Off the Head of Holofernes, by Artemisia Gentileschi,
17th century. *Uffizi Gallery, Florence*

Esther and Ahasuerus, by Artemisia Gentileschi, 17th century.
Metropolitan Museum of Art, New York

surpasses most of them in power of expression and dramatic intensity, which are usually thought of as peculiarly male characteristics. In fact, she was a most extraordinary woman in both her art and her life. In her youth, her father took legal action against his friend and colleague Agostino Tassi who, according to the charges, had repeatedly raped his daughter. She later married the Florentine Pietro Antonio Schiattesi, but there is a record showing that she was separated from him, and in a letter she inquired if he was still alive. Other aspects of her life, such as the affairs she is supposed to have had with a variety of men, including a priest, all added to her rather scandalous reputation.

Much has been made by modern commentators of the possible relationship between her life, especially her rape at an early age, and the violent subject matter that she chose. However, in light of the fact that R. Ward Bissell's research[9] shows that Artemisia was not sixteen but nineteen at the time of the trial and that it was charged that the violation of the girl took place over and over again, it would seem that Tassi's contention that the young lady was not that innocent cannot be completely ignored. Nevertheless, the kinds of women she portrayed may well reflect a basic hostility toward men. Favorite subjects, repeatedly shown in the most gory detail with violent action and dramatic contrasts of light and dark, were Judith cutting off the head of Holofernes and Esther, the Jewish heroine, plotting the destruction of her enemy

[9]R. Ward Bissell, "Artemisia Gentileschi—A New Documented Chronology," *Art Bulletin* (June 1968), vol. 50, pp. 153–68.

Haman. Others were Lucretia killing herself after being violated by Tarquinius, Susanna falsely accused by the Elders, Bathsheba taken by David, and Mary Magdalene, the fallen woman who became a saint. The female heroine, always presented as a powerful and sensuous person, was a recurrent theme in her work, or at least in many of her most important paintings, for she did, of course, do canvases dealing with more conventional subjects and she also made numerous portraits. Her early work is forceful and extremely realistic, embodying the essence of the Caravaggesque ideals, while her later work tends to be less violent, no doubt reflecting the changing taste of the period during which the more classical style of the Bolognese school became more popular. But Artemisia never lost the vigor of her brushwork or the dramatic intensity of her style during the four decades she was active as an artist. There is no doubt that she must be looked upon as the greatest woman painter Italy has produced and one of the outstanding artists of her period, a fact which has been recognized only in recent times, since earlier critics often underrated her because they had puritanical scruples about her life.

In the north of Europe, the Dutch School was dominant in the seventeenth century, and it is among the Dutch painters that the leading female artists appeared. Outstanding were Judith Leyster and Rachel Ruysch, but many others could also be mentioned. Most of them were minor artists working in a restricted genre like flower and still-life painting, usually in a style derived from some better-known man with whom they had studied. At their best, however, they are very accomplished painters whose work is equal to that of all but the greatest Dutch masters, and several were highly regarded by their contemporaries. As in Italy, most of them were either the daughters of painters or they were married to fellow artists, which made it easier for them to follow their artistic inclinations in a society that continued to be prejudiced against women artists.

Judith Leyster, the elder of the two, was born in Haarlem in 1609 and died there in 1660. In 1636 she married a fellow painter, Jan Molenaer, with whom she lived for a time in Amsterdam. The greatest influence on her work was Frans Hals, whose pupil she became at the age of twenty. Like her teacher, she specialized in figure compositions painted in a very lively and loose style. Her best pictures are works of real merit although they have little originality. Her professional competence was widely acclaimed and she became a member of the guild of Saint Luke of her native city. Rachel Ruysch was born in Amsterdam in 1664, the daughter of a famous professor of anatomy. She studied with the well-known flower painter Willem van Aelst, and devoted herself exclusively to this genre. She married the painter Juriaen Pool, with whom she had ten children. Although she had a long life, dying in 1750 at the age of eighty-six, her output was small and her work is rather rare today. She enjoyed great fame during her lifetime, and prices as high as one thousand florins were paid for her pictures. Among her particular patrons was the Elector of the Palatinate, who made her his court painter and bought many of her pictures, some of which he presented to the Grand Duke of Tuscany. Mrs. Ellet, in *Women Artists,* says that "she carried flower painting to

>

Self-portrait, by Judith Leyster, 17th century. *National Gallery, Washington, D.C.*

A HISTORY OF WOMEN ARTISTS

Flowers, by Rachel Ruysch, 18th century. *Metropolitan Museum of Art, New York*

a perfection never before attained" and Jean-Baptiste Descampes, the art critic, felt that her flowers and fruits "surpassed nature herself." Such praise is exaggerated, but her canvases depict flowers and fruits in a very detailed and realistic manner, giving a perfect illusion of nature and often achieving very beautiful effects. While certainly a minor artist, she achieved perfection within the limitations she imposed.

Anna Maria Schurman, who lived from 1607 to 1678, was of Flemish parentage, although born in Cologne where her parents were Protestant refugees. A most gifted and remarkable woman not only as an artist but as a linguist and scholar, Anna Maria began to read at three, could speak Latin at seven, and by ten translated a passage of Seneca from Latin into French and Flemish. At the same time she began painting birds and flowers, an art that she taught herself. Loving the study of languages above everything else, she soon mastered Greek and later embarked upon the study of Oriental languages. She is said to have spoken and written Hebrew, Samaritan, Arabic, Chaldaic, Syrian, Ethiopian, Turkish, and Persian, besides being perfectly acquainted with Italian,

A HISTORY OF WOMEN ARTISTS

Self-portrait, by Anna Maria Schurman, 17th century. *Collection of City Hall, Franeker, Holland*

Spanish French, English, and German.[10] By the age of eleven, she had read the Bible, Seneca, Virgil, Homer, and Aeschylus in the original and had composed an ode in Latin and verses in many languages. At the University of Leyden, a city in which her family had settled after their return to the Netherlands in 1615, she was always welcome and was often consulted by eminent scholars.

In addition to her amazing achievements as a linguist, Anna Maria Schurman also developed into a remarkable, many-sided artist whose talents and accomplishments were much admired. She excelled in drawing and painting, carved in wood and ivory, and modeled in wax. She also did copper engravings, producing some very fine prints, and she played several musical instruments. Particularly fine is her sensitive self-portrait painted in a very vivid and realistic style in keeping with the dominant

[10]E. Ellet, *Women Artists in All Ages and Countries* (New York: Harper & Bros., 1859), p. 100.

Flower with Butterfly and Caterpillar, by Maria Sibylla Merian, 18th century. *Collection of Oeffentlichen Kunstsammlung, Basel*

Flower and Butterfly, by Maria Sibylla Merian, 18th century. *Collection of Oeffentlichen Kunstsammlung, Basel*

manner of contemporary Dutch art. While it could not be said that she made a distinctive contribution to art or exerted an influence on later artists, she certainly is an outstanding example of how, by the seventeenth century, a gifted woman could establish herself and be accepted as an equal in the world of arts and letters.

Maria Sibylla Merian is another female artist who was probably more impressive for her total life and her versatility than for her artistic achievements. Born in Frankfurt in 1647, she came from a well-known family of printmakers and goldsmiths who had originated in Basel but had been active in Germany and Holland for many years. She married the German painter Johann Andreas Graff, with whom she moved to Nürnberg. She received her early instruction in painting from her stepfather Jacob Marrel and the famous flower painter Abraham Mignons. Working in oil and watercolor, she specialized in painting plants, fruits, and animals, using a very detailed,

A HISTORY OF WOMEN ARTISTS

realistic style. Her studies of plants and insects combined scientific accuracy with beauty of drawing. Encouraged by the success of her efforts, she published in 1679 a work called *The Wonderful Transformation of Caterpillars,* a quarto volume, with copper engravings based on her own drawings and watercolors. A second volume followed in 1684, the year she left her husband and returned to her native city of Frankfurt. But her scientific curiosity led her to the West Indies, her particular interest being the insects of Dutch Guiana, also called Surinam, specimens of which she had seen in Holland where she had become acquainted with professor Fredericus Ruysch, the father of painter Rachel Ruysch. Aided by the Dutch government, she undertook the lengthy and difficult journey to Surinam in 1699 and remained there for two years collecting specimens and studying the fauna and flora. The result was another splendid publication, *Metamorphosis Insectorum Surinamensium.* Her sketches of caterpillars, butterflies, spiders, snakes, and various kinds of animals and plants were rendered in engravings nearly the size of the originals. Her final work was *History of Insects of Europe, Drawn from Nature, and Explained by Maria Sibylla Merian.* It included a treatise on the generation and metamorphosis of insects and the plants on which they fed. The illustrations were executed with great fidelity and yet at the same time are beautiful works of art that can be enjoyed for their aesthetic merit. In this way, it might be said that her contribution to descriptive, scientifically inspired drawings is not unlike that of the French-born American artist Audubon whose depiction of North American birds became a classic. Merian died in 1717 in Amsterdam.

In France, the outstanding woman painter of the seventeenth century was Louise Moillon. Born in Paris in 1610, her father and brother were painters, and she began her artistic career at an early age. Her special interest was still life, and she anticipated the kind of formal composition associated with the work of Chardin and, later, Cézanne. Her arrangements of fruits and vegetables combine a detached and meticulous observation with an almost classical severity, achieving very simple but beautiful effects. Particularly fine is her sense of form with clearly defined light used to model the shapes. Although relatively little is known about her life and work, some twenty-five paintings dated between 1629 and 1682 are extant, and they clearly place her in the forefront of the women painters of her day. She died at age eighty-six in Paris in 1696.

It is difficult to choose among the many other women artists who were active during the late seventeenth and early eighteenth century, for there were hundreds of them in various European countries, many of whom achieved a considerable reputation during their lives. But there is at least one other who deserves individual treatment, and that is Anna Waser of Zurich, whom the Swiss consider one of their outstanding painters. Coming from a prominent patrician family, she showed great promise as an artist at a very early age and at thirteen made such an excellent copy of a painting by her teacher Joseph Werner that it was evident she was destined to be an artist. Her self-portrait, painted at the age of fifteen, now in the Kunsthaus in Zurich, is one of her most outstanding achievements. Her particular interest was in miniature painting, a branch in which many women excelled. Her fame as a portrait painter and draftsman was so great that her work was taken to Germany, Holland, and England, and she received many commissions from German courts. Particularly moving are the very expressive pencil drawings of her later years, such as the one showing her as a lovely young woman in the company of death. In fact, this sketch was prophetic, for in 1713 she died in the midst of a brilliant career, her life cut short at the age of thirty-four.

Still Life, by Louise Moillon, 17th century. *Private collection, New York*

Fruit basket, by Louise Moillon, 17th century. *Courtesy Parke-Bernet Gallery*

Self-portrait, by Anna Waser, 17th century. *Collection of Kunsthaus, Zurich*

4 WOMEN PAINTERS OF THE EIGHTEENTH CENTURY

A MARKED change in the position of women took place in the eighteenth century. Spurred by the liberal ideals of the age of enlightenment, women became far more important in the cultural life of the time, and the leading women artists enjoyed a success and fame equal to that of the most celebrated of their male counterparts. The great French thinkers such as Voltaire and Rousseau served as a liberating force, and Addison and Steele in their magazines, *The Tatler* and *The Spectator,* advocated a greater role for women, emphasizing that their periodicals addressed themselves to women as well as men for it was women who had to civilize society. As Professor A. R. Humphreys says in his essay on the social setting of the eighteenth century in England:

> The humanitarian philosophy with its concern for personality involved, too, a growing respect for women. . . . As the years passed, women played an increasingly important part in social life, which improved markedly in moral tone and politeness, and in the constitution of the reading public. The later eighteenth century is noted for the expression of feminine taste through the Blue-stocking salons of ladies like Mrs. Vesey, Mrs. Boscawen and the famous Mrs. Montagu, and the literary activities of others like Elizabeth Carter (who translated Epictetus to general admiration), Mrs. Thrale (Dr. Johnson's hostess and friend), and Fanny Burney.[11]

[11]B. Ford, *The Pelican Guide to English Literature* (London, 1957), vol. 4, p. 45.

In France women like Madame de Staël and Rousseau's friend Mme. d'Épinay were prominent in intellectual life, and philosophers like Condorcet in his *Sketch for a historical picture of the progress of the human mind* of 1793–1794 not only advocated the liberation of mankind from ignorance, tyranny, and superstition by means of science and reason but also favored universal education and equality of the sexes. The most astonishing figure in this field is the English writer Mary Wollstonecraft who, in *A Vindication of the Rights of Women* of 1792, presented views so extreme that they still seemed radical a century later. Her book was dedicated to the French statesman Talleyrand in order to persuade him to grant women equal educational opportunities in the new French Republic. Addressing herself to Talleyrand, she chides him for treating the rights of women in "too cursory a manner, contented to consider it as it had been considered formerly, when the rights of man, not to advert to women, were trampled on as chimerical. I call upon you, therefore, now to weigh what I have advanced requesting the rights of woman, and natural education—and I call with the firm tone of humanity. For my arguments, Sir, are dedicated by a disinterested spirit—I plead for my sex—not for myself."[12] She advocated complete equality for women, equal educational opportunities, and freedom from the drudgery of housework and from gaining a place in the world solely by being attractive to men. Although she was a pioneer far ahead of her time, Mary Wollstonecraft reflects the profound change which was taking place during the second half of the eighteenth century when the ideals of the American and the French revolutions led to greater liberty, equality, and fraternity not only for men but for women as well.

The result of the emancipation of women and their greater participation in cultural life was a marked increase in the number of women active in the arts. The earlier female artists had been largely the daughters or wives of male artists, but now they were often from families that had no artistic connections or else they had fathers whose fame they eclipsed, as was the case with Elisabeth Vigée-Lebrun and Angelica Kauffmann, both daughters of minor artists who are totally forgotten today. Just how many women were working as painters, engravers, sculptors, and in the various decorative arts has never been established, but they must have numbered in the thousands, with the most illustrious rivaling the best of their male contemporaries.

Eighteenth-century France took the lead in women artists, but Germany, Switzerland, Italy, England, Holland, Belgium, Spain, and Poland, as well as the Scandinavian countries produced female painters of note. Even Russia under Catherine the Great proved hospitable to women artists, for when Elisabeth Vigée-Lebrun was exiled as a Royalist from her native France, she was welcomed at the court of Saint Petersburg, where she remained for a number of years. There was also a marked change in the social position of women artists, which is evident in the fact that Vigée-Lebrun was an intimate of Queen Marie Antoinette and Catherine the Great, while Angelica Kauffmann was a friend of Goethe's and the British royal family.

The earliest of these outstanding women painters was Rosalba Carriera, an Italian artist who was born in Venice in 1675. Her father, a government official who had once been a painter, encouraged his daughter to pursue an artistic career after she had shown great promise as a child. She studied under the well-known painter Antonio Nazari and, later, under Giuseppe Diamantini and Antonio Balestra. Her works,

[12]M. Wollstonecraft, *A Vindication of the Rights of Women* (London, 1792), p. 7.

Portrait of a Lady with Laurel Wreath,
by Rosalba Carriera, 18th century.
Museum of Fine Arts, Boston

especially those in pastel, were admired all over Europe, and she was referred to as the "companion of the muse of painting" and "the ornament of her sex and of the Venetian school." In fact, her fame was so great that she was invited to Paris and Vienna, two of the outstanding art capitals of the time, and the art academies of Paris, Bologna, and Rome elected her to their memberships. Emperor Charles of Austria, the King of France, the Grand Duke of Tuscany, and Augustus, king of Poland and elector of Saxony, sat for their portraits, and the most illustrious men and the most beautiful women of Europe vied with one another to have themselves painted by her. The brothers Goncourt in their book on French eighteenth-century painters give the following account of Rosalba's sojourn in Paris. In speaking of Maurice Quentin de la Tour, they say:

And it is possible that the presence of Rosalba in Paris in 1720, and again in 1721, may have had some influence on his vocation. La Tour might have witnessed that triumph of the art of pastel, the great success of the Venetian pastellist who was visited by the Regent, sought after by the highest aristocracy, crushed beneath money and commission, from whom such women as Mesdames Parabere and de Prie solicited, implored their portraits, enthralled by the charm of her art which somehow contrived to invest the female face with a vague, cloud-like insubstantiality, the breath of a resemblance exhaled from a bouquet of color.[13]

After a glorious career, her later life was clouded with tragedy. At the age of fifty, she became totally blind, and although she lived on until 1757, her closing years were ones of complete withdrawal and artistic inactivity.

By far the most famous eighteenth-century woman painter, and the most celebrated of all female artists up to that time, was Marie Anne Elisabeth Vigée. Born in Paris in 1755, she showed such marked talent as a girl that she was encouraged by her father, who was a minor painter. After her father's early death, she studied with Briard. Success came early, for already at sixteen the well-known painter Joseph Vernet admired her work and sought out the young artist, who was also very beautiful and charming. Recalling this period in her memoirs, Vigée-Lebrun says:

> From the age of sixteen I had mixed in the best society, and knew all our first artists, so that I received invitations from all quarters. I remember very well dining the first time in Paris with Le Moine, the sculptor, then very renowned. He was a man of great simplicity; but he had the good taste to bring together at his house a number of celebrated and distinguished characters; his two daughters did the honors perfectly.[14]

Walking one day in the park of the château at Marly-le-Roi, she encountered for the first time the French queen, who was to play such a great role in her life.

> It was there that I met one morning Queen Marie Antoinette, who was walking in the park with several of her court ladies. All were in white dresses, and were so young and pretty that they looked like apparitions. I was with my mother, and we were retreating from them when the Queen had the goodness to stop, and desired me to continue my promenade wherever I pleased.

Using a fashionable style that combined the grace of Rococo with the simplicity of Neo-Classicism, Vigée-Lebrun went from triumph to triumph and soon became the most sought after portrait painter in Paris. Queen Marie Antoinette invited the young woman to Versailles to paint her portrait, and the two became lifelong friends. In 1783, when she was only twenty-eight years old, she was invited to become a member of the Academy, sponsored by Joseph Vernet. She was admitted on the basis of a canvas she painted especially for the occasion, an allegorical work in a classical style which is called *Peace Bringing Back Abundance.* In the meantime she had married the art dealer Jean-Baptiste Lebrun, a union that was not very happy and was dissolved thirteen years later. After her marriage she called herself Elisabeth Vigée-Lebrun, the name by which she has become world famous.

With the advent of the French Revolution in 1789, all this came to an abrupt end. A friend of the queen and a staunch Royalist, Vigée-Lebrun was forced to leave France, going first to Rome, where she met Angelica Kauffmann and was asked by the Pope to paint his portrait. From Rome she went to Naples where she painted the royal court,

[13]E. & J. De Goncourt, *French XVIII Century Painters* (London, 1848), pp. 162–63.
[14]*Souvenirs of Madame Vigée-Lebrun* (New York, 1889), pp. 24–25.

then on to Vienna, Saint Petersburg, and Berlin, finally returning to Paris in 1801. After a brief stay in France, she moved to England where she remained until 1805 when she returned to France for good. She died in Paris in 1842, but the later part of her career was less distinguished. Wherever she went she was received with great honor, and the aristocrats were eager to have their portraits painted by the illustrious artist. The great skill that she showed in her work and the graceful elegance with which she portrayed her sitters won her friends and admirers all over Europe, and as a result she enjoyed a reputation unequaled by any female artist of earlier times and unsurpassed by any since. Her self-portraits are particularly fine, especially those showing the artist with her daughter Julie. While her portraits are very accomplished and give a vivid picture of the aristocracy of the late eighteenth century, modern critics usually find them too pretty and superficial. They are skillful, certainly pleasing, but they lack the depth and greatness that the portraits of her contemporary Goya possessed.

Her chief rival and in some ways an even better painter was Adélaïde Labille-Guiard (1749–1803). The daughter of a cloth merchant, she married a neighbor, a Monsieur Guiard, from whom she was separated after a few years. She studied pastel under the aged Maurice Quentin de La Tour and miniature painting under François Vincent, with whose son André, who had also been her teacher, she lived for many years. She finally married him in 1800, just three years before her death. Unlike Vigée-Lebrun, who usually painted feminine subjects treated in a soft, delicate style, Labille-Guiard's work had greater strength and firmness. It was often characterized as masculine, and some critics even doubted that she painted her own pictures—they did not think that a woman could have created them. However, she triumphed over the sceptics and was elected to the Royal Academy in 1783, the same year as Vigée-Lebrun, after she had demonstrated her talent by painting portraits of the members of the academy. In fact, it was in her portraits that her greatest gift lay. This was recognized

Daughter of the Artist, by Elisabeth Vigée-Lebrun, 18th century. *Museum of Fine Arts, Boston*

The Marquise de Pezé and the Marquise de Rouget with Her Two Children, by
Elisabeth Vigée-Lebrun, 18th century. *National Gallery, Washington, D.C.*

Madame Grand, by Elisabeth Vigée-Lebrun, 18th century.
Metropolitan Museum of Art, New York

in her lifetime, for Louis XVI named her official painter to the Mesdames of France, his three maiden aunts. Her portraits were much admired but, since she lacked the beauty and social charm of Vigée-Lebrun, she was less successful, and she has tended to be unduly neglected by posterity because she was overshadowed by her glamorous rival. Modern critics, however, have acknowledged her very real merit, and "only now is she being rediscovered as one of the great artists of the century."[15] This rediscovery may be partially due to the fact that, unlike Vigée-Lebrun, who was a Royalist and courtier, Labille-Guiard was a more independent woman who remained in Paris after the Revolution, taught young women who wished to become painters, and challenged the rule that only men could be professors at the art academies.

If there has been any woman artist whose fame and success equaled that of Elisabeth Vigée-Lebrun, it was Angelica Kauffmann, who was born in 1741 and died in 1807. Her triumphs are reminiscent of the adulation enjoyed by the geniuses of the Renaissance, with not only royalty and cardinals but also artistic and literary figures like Canova, Johann Joachim Winckelmann, and Goethe singing her praises. As her biographer says of the time she met Goethe in Rome:

> Angelica was the popular painter in Rome, styled the Mother of the Arts, and in many respects the most popular person, at that time, in the whole city, because she was noted, not only for her painting, but also for her brilliant conversation, and her skill in music, so that her studio was crowded with admiring patrons, all of whom were anxious to sit for her, or to purchase some of her popular classical pictures.[16]

She was besieged by art patrons from all over Europe who wished to acquire her paintings. Even when she was ill, the number of commissions was so large that she asked if she were not even permitted to be sick. "Are there not painters besides myself?" she said, and it is reported that the reply was "No, none, and when you stop creating, art will be orphaned."[17] At least four nations claimed the honor of counting her as their own—Switzerland, where she was born; Germany, since her father came from the Lake Constance region; England, where she spent some of the most productive years of her life; and Italy, which was her true home and where she is buried in the Pantheon along with Raphael and other immortals. When she died, she left a quarter of a million crowns, which she had earned from her paintings, a splendid villa, an extensive library, and an art collection that included the work of painters like Titian, Correggio, Van Dyck, and even Leonardo. Her popularity was so great that six hundred engravings were made after her work.

Born in Chur in eastern Switzerland in 1741, Angelica Kauffmann was the daughter of a minor painter who had come from the small village of Schwarzenberg near Bregenz in western Austria. However, when she was a child her father moved to Italy, first to Morbegno in Lombardy, where he received a commission, and later to Como, which Angelica always recalled with great fondness as the place where she spent some of the happiest years of her youth. When she was thirteen, the family moved to Milan,

[15]A. Gabhard and E. Brown, "Old Mistresses, Women Artists of the Past," *Bulletin of the Walters Art Gallery,* vol. 29, no. 7 (1972).
[16]V. Manners & G. C. Williamson, *Angelica Kauffmann* (New York and London, 1924), p. 67.
[17]R. Muther, *Geschichte der Malerei,* vol. 3 (Leipzig, 1930), p. 117.

>

Portrait of the Artist with Two Pupils, by Adélaïde Labille-Guiard, 18th century. *Metropolitan Museum of Art, New York*

Self-portrait, by Angelica Kauffmann, 18th century. *Galleria dell'Accademia di San Luca, Rome*

Joachim Winckelmann, by Angelica Kauffmann, 18th century. *Collection of Kunsthaus, Zurich*

where she first saw paintings by old masters, which she was permitted to copy. After the death of her mother in 1757, Angelica and her father returned to his native village where he was asked to decorate the local church, a task in which his young daughter assisted him. Angelica was not only a talented painter, whose gift had been evident since childhood, she was also a beautiful girl who was as accomplished in music as in art and who spoke fluent Italian, German, French, and English. After a few years father and daughter returned to Italy, first to Milan, then to Parma and Bologna and, finally, in 1763, when she was twenty-one, Angelica arrived in Rome which, with the exception of her stay in England, became her true home. The German archaeologist Winckelmann, who met her at this time and had his portrait painted by her, describes her thus in a letter to a friend:

> I have just been painted by a stranger, a young person of rare merit. She is very eminent in portraits in oil, mine is half-length, and she has made an etching of it as a present to me. She speaks Italian as well as German, and expresses herself with the

Painters of the Eighteenth Century

Holy Family, by Angelica Kauffmann, 18th century. *Collection of Kunsthaus, Zurich*

same facility in French and English, on which account she paints all the English who visit Rome. She sings with taste which ranks her among our greatest virtuosi. Her name is Angelica Kauffmann.[18]

After several years in Rome, Naples, and Venice, Angelica was urged by the wife of the British ambassador to come to England where she predicted great success for the young woman. She arrived in London in 1766 when she was twenty-five years old and immediately caused a great sensation. She was courted by Sir Joshua Reynolds, at that time the most influential painter in England. The nobility flocked to her studio to have their portraits painted and the Royal Academy invited her to become one of its founding members. In addition to the numerous portrait commissions she received, she was also

[18]Manners and Williamson, *Angelica Kauffmann* (New York and London, 1924) p. 14.

A HISTORY OF WOMEN ARTISTS

asked to paint part of the decorations of Saint Paul's church in London, as well as the ceiling designs for the vestibule of the Royal Academy. The royal family itself honored her with its patronage and the queen became a personal friend. Her only misfortune was that she was tricked into marriage by an impostor who posed as a Swedish nobleman but turned out to be his German butler. However, the marriage was soon annulled and it in no way dimmed her brilliant career.

At the age of forty, after fifteen years in England, she married an Italian painter, Antonio Zucchi, with whom she returned to Italy and settled in Rome, where she spent the rest of her life. It was here that the young Goethe became infatuated with her, that Winckelmann instructed her in classical mythology and art, and that Elisabeth Vigée-Lebrun visited her in 1789, pronouncing her "interesting apart from her talents, on account of her intelligence, and her knowledge." Her husband, who was somewhat older than she, vastly admired her and devoted his entire life to serving his wife by taking care of the household, purchasing canvas and frames, and tending to business affairs. Her life as a result was very happy, devoted wholly to her work and to the stimulating social and intellectual group of which she was a center. Certainly no woman artist has ever achieved such a position or enjoyed such unbroken success, which lasted until she died in 1807, aged sixty-six years.

When one turns to Angelica Kauffmann's work, the modern critic is at a loss to explain her extraordinary fame. In fact, it must be said that Elisabeth Vigée-Lebrun's painting has worn rather better than that of her famous contemporary. Walter Sparrow, writing in 1905 and reflecting a Victorian sensibility, says that she "is quite artificial in spirit, with a strong bias towards the sentimental," although he does grant her "considerable charm and ability." But he adds, "In recent times Angelica Kauffmann has been remembered for the romance of her personal life and treated with cool contempt in all that appertains to her work." In explaining this, he says that "critics have searched in her pictures for many qualities and, finding there the temperament of a sentimental woman, their judgement has failed them."[19] More recent critics have come to the conclusion that her friends and contemporaries in England—Reynolds, Gainsborough, and Benjamin West—all outrank her and that, today, her work seems "sentimental, or overdone, or the portraits themselves dark." However, the authors of this passage add that her paintings should not be so considered, and that "as achievements they are outstanding."[20]

The truth of the matter, as so often in art history, seems to lie somewhere between the high esteem she enjoyed during her life and the neglect she has suffered in recent times. Certainly part of her success was due to her beauty and vivacity, which were praised by all who encountered her. Yet, there can be no doubt that she was an accomplished and versatile painter whose output was prodigious and who had a remarkable ability to conform to the prevailing taste. But it was just this quality that has hurt her reputation—that is, her tremendous facility in turning out Neo-Classical scenes in the style of Anton Mengs and elegant portraits of the English court in the manner of Reynolds. Her portraits stand up best, whereas her more ambitious allegorical compositions with their empty and sentimental heroics have little appeal to modern taste.

[19]W. Sparrow, *Women Painters,* pp. 58–59.
[20]W. & F. Neilson, *Seven Women: Great Painters* (Philadelphia, 1969), p. 21.

5 WOMEN PAINTERS OF THE NINETEENTH CENTURY

THE TREND toward the emancipation of women increased during the nineteenth century. Mrs. Ellet writing in 1859 reports that "the progress of female talent and skill, accelerated towards the close of the preceding age, has become more remarkable than ever within the last fifty years. The number of women engaged in the pursuit of art during that time far exceeds that of the whole preceding century." She goes on to say that while this may be partially due to the greater general appreciation of the arts, it is also "due in some degree, to the increased freedom of women—to her liberation from the thraldom of old-fashioned prejudices and unworthy restraints which, in former times, fettered her energies, rendered her acquisition of scientific and artistic knowledge extremely difficult, and threw obstacles in the way of her devotion to study and the exercise of her talents."[21]

Not only did the number of women artists increase, but the recognition they received was also correspondingly greater although, interestingly enough, none of them achieved the kind of personal success that Vigée-Lebrun and Angelica Kauffmann had enjoyed at the turn of the century. An indication of this development is found in the Paris salons in which there were 25 women out of 180 exhibitors in 1800 and 46 out of 311 in 1808; by 1831, just one generation later, no less than 149 of the 873 painters were female.

[21]E. Ellet, *Women Artists,* p. 234.

‹

Mlle. Charlotte de Val d'Ognes, by Constance-Marie Charpentier, 19th century.
Metropolitan Museum of Art, New York

The greater opportunity for women artists was especially noticeable in the United States, where women had previously played a very minor role. They began to attend art schools and exhibit their work in major museums and galleries. The most advanced country in this respect was France, where, by the middle of the nineteenth century, one quarter of all practicing artists were women. Yet, there were still formidable barriers against female artists. The great centers of art education like the École des Beaux-Arts remained closed to them, and society at large as well as many parents still disapproved of young women pursuing an art career in any but an amateur way. There were also reservations about giving women major commissions and official prizes, although here, too, women were making considerable progress. By the end of the century, Walter Sparrow felt compelled to add a note to his book on women painters, apologizing for the thousands of gifted contemporary artists he was forced to leave out.

This great outpouring of female painting was not restricted to a few countries nor was it limited to any particular style, but it was a trend that occurred in all Western countries and schools of art. While many leading women artists of earlier times had specialized in portrait painting, the full range of subjects was now mastered by women, and every major artistic movement—Classicism, Romanticism, Realism, Impressionism—had its female practitioners who (while never equaling the best male artists) achieved results that compare favorably with the work of their male colleagues.

While Vigée-Lebrun lived well into the nineteenth century, dying in 1842, the kind of elegant court painting she produced ceased to be important after the French Revolution. The new leading artist was Jacques Louis David whose Neo-Classical canvases were believed to be more in keeping with the democratic ideals of the new republic. Among his most gifted students was a young woman artist, Constance-Marie Charpentier. She was born in Paris in 1767 and died there in 1841. In addition to studying under David, whose work had a formative influence on her style, she also studied with various other artists, notably Gérard. Although few of her works are known today, records show that she was a regular contributor to the salons, showing some thirty canvases in ten exhibitions between the years 1795 and 1819. The subjects seem to have been portraits, allegories like *Melancholy* in the Amiens Museum, and genre scenes such as *The First Cure of the Young Doctor* and *A Mother Receiving the Confidence of Her Daughter,* both of which were exhibited in the salons.

Her most famous painting, upon which her reputation largely rests today, is a picture that for many years was attributed to David, namely, her portrait of Charlotte de Val d'Ognes, now in the Metropolitan Museum in New York. Acquired by the museum in 1917, it was looked upon for many years as one of the outstanding works of David in America, but it was reattributed to Madame Charpentier by the French art historian Charles Sterling, on the basis of its style and documentary evidence showing conclusively that David could not have painted it. *Art News* calls it "perhaps the greatest picture ever painted by a woman." While this claim may be excessive, there is no doubt that it is the work of an exceptional artist. Combining the classical composition of David with the softer modeling of Gérard, she created a style all her own, which has a beautiful serenity and a kind of cool radiance in which the darks and lights are sensitively played against each other.

Another outstanding woman painter who studied with David and also Vigée-Lebrun was Marie Guilhelmine Benoist, who was born in Paris in 1768 and died there in 1826. She showed two pictures in the Salon of 1791, one of which was called *Psyche's Farewell*

Marie Pauline Bonaparte, by Marie Guilhelmine Benoist,
19th century. *Collection of Versailles Palace*

from Her Family and the other of which was a scene from Richardson's novel *Clarissa Harlowe.* However, her best work is her portraits, the finest of which is a magnificent picture of a Negress, now in the collection of the Louvre, which was first exhibited in the Salon of 1800. It combines the firmness of David's drawing and composition with a vivid lifelike quality that is masterful. She also painted several portraits of Napoleon and a well-known picture of Pauline Borghese, the last now at Versailles. However, these official portraits lack the warmth and vitality of her more informal work.

Somewhat younger is Constance Mayer, the third outstanding woman painter of early nineteenth-century Paris. Although she had a brilliant career, she committed suicide in 1821, at the age of forty-three. Her teacher and, later, lover was Prud'hon, who introduced her to a softer, more romantic style. In keeping with this influence, her work is more poetic and sentimental than that of Charpentier or Benoist. Pictures like *The Deserted Mother, A Dream of Happiness,* and *Venus and Cupid Asleep Caressed and Awakened by Zephyr* are characteristic of her subject matter. Although it is said that she worshiped Prud'hon and that he actually helped her in much of her work, there is a dreamy quality about her painting that is quite her own. Her death was very much in character with her strongly emotional nature for, feeling that Prud'hon no longer loved her, she killed herself in front of his eyes.

The best-known woman painter of the nineteenth century was Rosa Bonheur who, at the time of her death in 1899, was one of the most celebrated and successful artists of

The Horse Fair, by Rosa Bonheur, 19th century. *Metropolitan Museum of Art, New York*

the period. Her naturalistic animal paintings were far more popular than any of the works of the Impressionists or Post-Impressionists, and her large canvas *The Horse Fair,* first shown at the Paris Salon of 1853, continues to be one of the most popular paintings in New York's Metropolitan Museum. No doubt her great appeal lay not just in the striking realism of the animals she painted, but in her emancipated life and her freedom from convention which is perhaps best exemplified by the fact that she usually wore trousers and an artist's smock instead of female dress. Walter Sparrow, writing about her shortly after her death, says:

> But the naturalist movement it was that witnessed the development of the greatest artistic personality in the feminine world of today—Rosa Bonheur. The role played by Rosa Bonheur is important from the feminine point of view, for the reason that she broke away from ancient traditions. She revealed what woman was capable of in the matter of energy, of continuity of purpose, of method, of scientific direction, in a word, in the indispensable impetus of inspiration. Before her day, the woman-painter had always been looked upon rather as a phenomenon, or her place in the domain of art was conceded to her on the grounds that she was indulging in an elevating and tasteful pastime, coming under the category of "accomplishments." Rosa Bonheur gave to woman a position equal to that of man.[22]

Born in Bordeaux in 1822, she was the daughter of a painter and drawing instructor and had two brothers who also became artists. From an early age, she showed a remarkable talent for drawing and much preferred sketching the woods and animals to attending school. Her father was an ardent disciple of Saint Simon, the utopian religious and social reformer who believed in the coming of a woman Messiah and favored complete equality for women. It has been suggested that, because of this influence, she was led to believe in her youth that women should make their own way. As she herself said, "I have no patience with women who ask permission to think. Let women establish their claims by great and good works, and not by conventions." Working first in her father's studio and then in the Louvre, the young artist showed such remarkable talent that an elderly Englishman, observing her in the Louvre, told her that he predicted she would become a great artist. At first she painted landscapes, genre scenes, and historical canvases, but she found her true subject when she discovered animal painting, and after that she could not be kept from visiting the animals and museum of the Jardin des Plantes, the stables of the veterinary school, and the slaughterhouses of Paris. In 1841, when she was only nineteen years old, she made her debut at the Paris Salon with a charming little picture of a goat, sheep, and rabbits. The following year she exhibited three pictures, *Animals in Pasture, A Cow Lying in a Meadow,* and *A Horn for Sale.* Her success was immediate and her entries won bronze and silver medals. In 1849, when she was only twenty-seven, she was awarded the much coveted gold medal for her *Cantal Oxen,* with the famous painter Vernet, the president of the awards committee, proclaiming her the new laureate.

Rosa Bonheur went from triumph to triumph. *Plowing in Nivernais* of 1848, ordered by the government and now hanging in the Louvre, *The Horse Fair* of 1853, and *Hay Making* of 1855 were enthusiastically acclaimed by the public. Among her most ardent admirers were the British and the Americans, who found her love of animals and her straightforward realism very appealing. While the success of Elisabeth

[22]Sparrow, *Women Painters,* pp. 180–81.

A HISTORY OF WOMEN ARTISTS

Vigée-Lebrun and Angelica Kauffmann had been more with the aristocracy and the connoisseurs, Rosa Bonheur was popular with the general public and crowds swarmed to see her work wherever it was exhibited. In fact, her *Horse Fair* was expressly bought at the high price of 40,000 francs in order to be shown for an admission charge. Even the Empress Eugénie came to see her paintings, as the artist relates in a letter to her brother and sister:

> I am happy to announce to you that yesterday I received the most gracious visit that a sovereign can pay to an artist, and that I am most deeply touched by it. Her Majesty came with all her Court to surprise me. You may fancy, my Juliette, how gladly I would, at first, have hidden myself in any mouse-hole. . . . I am going to paint a picture for the Empress. She gave me the order in the most charming manner, and I intend to do my best to execute it in a creditable fashion. As I was taking her to her carriage, she held out her hand to me, and I thought it my duty to kiss it. Thereupon, with the greatest kindness, this sovereign, whose simplicity and affability add to her distinction, did me the honor to embrace me. I don't think a higher mark of esteem and favor could have been shown me.[23]

In light of such adulation, it is difficult for the contemporary critic to assess Rosa Bonheur's true position in the history of art. Certainly the praises heaped upon her during her lifetime were much too extravagant, and there is no doubt that several of her male contemporaries, who were less successful at the time, have emerged as far greater artists. It is also true that she is surpassed by at least two women painters of the period, Berthe Morisot and Mary Cassatt. However, it may be that as the emphasis upon formal values declines—an emphasis that has dominated modern art criticism ever since the days of Meier-Graefe and Roger Fry—the narrative and naturalistic qualities of her work will again be appreciated.

Berthe Morisot's fate has been just the opposite of Rosa Bonheur's, for today her reputation is much higher than it was during her life. In fact, many critics would not hesitate to say that she is the best woman painter who has so far emerged. She herself would probably be surprised by the high regard in which she is held, just as Rosa Bonheur would be astonished to learn that her reputation had begun to decline at the very beginning of the twentieth century, only a few years after her death at seventy-seven, and that artists such as Cézanne and Van Gogh are considered far greater.

Unlike Rosa Bonheur, who had come from a poor artist's family, Berthe Morisot, who was born in 1841, was a member of the well-to-do bourgeoisie. At the time of her birth, her father was a prefect at Bourges, but later he was appointed to a government post in Paris. At seventeen Berthe and her sister Edma, who was also gifted but gave up painting after her marriage, took art lessons, first briefly from Chocarne and then from an artist named Guichard who was a follower of Delacroix. But it was her next teacher, Corot, who was the decisive influence in her artistic career. Corot, at this time a man of sixty-four, was a leading landscape painter in France, and it was from him that the young artist learned to paint outdoors, sketching the fields and woodlands of her native countryside. Working under Corot for a period of six years, Berthe Morisot formed her style and became an accomplished painter in her own right. By 1864, at the age of twenty-three, she was ready to exhibit at the Salon, where she showed two landscapes.

In 1868 she met Edouard Manet, an encounter that turned out to be the most

[23]T. Staunton, *Reminiscences of Rosa Bonheur* (New York, 1910), p. 96.

In the Dining Room, by Berthe Morisot,
19th century. *National Gallery, Washington, D.C.*

important in her life. At that time Manet was at the height of his fame. He had already shown his *Madame Olympia* and *Déjeuner sur l'Herbe,* which had created a public scandal, and he was a leading member of the artistic avant-garde. It was through Manet that the artist, now twenty-seven years old, met the writers Baudelaire, Mallarmé, and Zola, and the painters who would comprise the nucleus of the Impressionist movement. In fact, the Morisot and Manet families, both of whom belonged to the upper bourgeoisie, became very friendly, which ultimately led to Berthe's marriage in 1874 to Edouard's younger brother Eugene. Through Manet she learned to use looser and freer brushstrokes and to represent contemporary subjects, while she in turn led Manet to paint more out of doors. A visit to Spain in 1872 acquainted her with the work of Goya and Velásquez, both of whom she much admired, and whose styles of painting influenced her own.

By her early thirties, Berthe Morisot had fully developed her mature style and she joined the group of artists who were to be known as the Impressionists. In fact, Berthe Morisot was one of the painters who organized the first Impressionist exhibition at Nadar's Gallery in the spring of 1874. (The others were Monet, Pissarro, Sisley, Renoir, Degas, Cézanne, and Guillaumin.) Nine of her pictures were included in this first show,

Peruvian Indian Paracas Textile, circa 300 B.C.
Collection Merrin, New York

Collage No. 303, by Anne Ryan, circa 1950. *Collection Marlborough Gallery, New York*

◄ *Einödhof*, by Gabriele Münter, 1916. *Collection Leonard Hutton Gallery, New York*

Clearing, by Joan Mitchell, 1973. *Whitney Museum of American Art. Gift of Susan Morse Hilles in honor of John I. H. Baur*

Hommage à Chardin, by Helen Frankenthaler, 1957. *Collection Mr. and Mrs. Guy Weill, Scarsdale, New York*

Proserpine ou les Enfants Substitués, by Leonor Fini, 1973. *Collection L. Monet, Geneva, Switzerland*

Abstraction, by Sonia Delaunay, 1969. *Collection Virginia Field, New York*

New York Children, by Helen Levitt, 1973. *Collection of the artist*

The Mother and Sister of the Artist, by Berthe Morisot, 19th century. *National Gallery, Washington, D.C.*

and from then on she no longer sent any of her work to the Salon but became a regular member of the new school. In an auction of Impressionist paintings held the following year at the Hotel Drouet, it was her canvases that were most successful, in spite of the fact that Monet and Renoir were included. The second group show held, in 1876, contained twenty of her pictures and inspired the art critic of *Figaro* to say that "five or six lunatics, one of whom is a woman" were exhibiting their work.

Her life from then on continued serenely. She spent most of the year in Paris working in her studio, with summer vacations at the seashore and sometimes trips to the South in the winter. Her friends were mostly fellow artists, notably Degas, Monet, Renoir, and, later, Mary Cassatt. The great events in her personal life were the birth in 1878 of her daughter, Julie, who became one of her favorite subjects, and the death of her brother-in-law Edouard Manet in 1883 followed by the death of her husband in 1892. The Impressionist group exhibitions were followed by her first one-man show in Paris in 1892 and a show in New York. Her fame spread and, in 1894, official recognition came when one of her pictures was bought for the Luxembourg Museum. She died in 1895 at the age of fifty-four.

Almost eighty years have passed since Berthe Morisot's death, yet her position today is more secure than it was when she died. A large retrospective was held in 1941 at the Orangerie in Paris honoring the hundredth anniversary of her birth. In 1950 the Arts Council of Great Britain staged a one-man show of her work in London, and in 1952 there was a magnificent exhibition of the paintings of Berthe Morisot and her circle from the Rouart Collection, which traveled all over the United States and Canada. Numerous monographs about her life and her work have appeared in both French and English, and her collected letters have been published by her grandson Denis Rouart, the son of her daughter, Julie. Along with all the members of the original Impressionist group, she is considered one of the great figures in French nineteenth-century painting, and her work hangs beside that of her friends Manet, Monet, Degas, and Renoir in all the leading museums of the world.

In summing up her person and her art, no better words could be found than those of the poet Paul Valéry, who was related to her by marriage. Speaking of Tante Berthe, as she was called in his home, he says,

> Those who know and love the charm of her work are fully aware of the sober qualities of her life—a life of retired elegance—simple, single-minded, inwardly and passionately devoted to her work. They know that the true begetters of her taste and vision were the luminous painters whose art died out before David: that her friends and constant associates were Mallarmé, Degas, Renoir, Claude Monet, and very few others; that her noble and unrelenting aim was the highest and most refined art, of the kind which, by means of countless studies, produced and then pitilessly destroyed, consumes itself to attain the final, miraculous effect of instantaneous creation out of the void.[24]

A contemporary and friend of Berthe Morisot was the American painter Mary Cassatt. Born in Pittsburgh in 1844 and brought up in Philadelphia, she too came from a well-to-do upper-middle-class family and did not depend upon her art for a living. But, unlike Berthe Morisot, Mary Cassatt never married. A woman of strong character and great independence, she went her own way, rejecting the genteel life of a Philadelphia lady. She had a considerable influence on American art, not only as one of America's outstanding painters (in fact, in the eyes of most French critics "le grand peintre américain") but also as an influence on American taste. She advised Mrs. Havemeyer, who was her closest friend, to buy the Impressionists as well as Goya and El Greco, and because of her social connections (her brother was president of the Pennsylvania Railroad), she was able to persuade many other well-to-do collectors to buy works by contemporary French painters.

Growing up in a cultured family which often traveled in Europe, Mary Cassatt developed a keen interest in art. In 1861, at the age of seventeen, she decided to become a student at the Pennsylvania Academy of Fine Arts, America's oldest and most prestigious art school, founded in 1805 by the late-eighteenth-century portrait painter Charles Willson Peale. The academy was famous for its collection of plaster casts modeled after the ancients, and when Mary Cassatt entered as a student she was instructed in how to make drawings after the antique art and how to copy the old masters, which at that time was the standard curriculum. Interestingly enough, one of her fellow students was Thomas Eakins, whom many critics today regard as her chief rival in nineteenth-century American art.

After four years at the Pennsylvania Academy, it had become clear to her that if

---

[24]P. Valery, *Degas, Manet and Morisot* (New York, 1960), p. 123.

she was serious about art, she would have to go to Europe, and in 1866, when she was twenty-two years old, her father gave her his reluctant permission. She traveled in Italy, Spain, Belgium, and Holland, where she studied the old masters and developed her own style. In 1873, she settled in Paris where she had already shown a picture in the Salon of the previous year. The decisive event of her life that was to influence all her later art was her introduction to Degas, who was brought to her studio by a friend and who liked her work so much that he invited her to join the Impressionist group. She became a leading member and one of the most ardent champions of the Impressionists, and her relationship to Degas developed into a lifelong friendship. Mary Cassatt was included in the fourth Impressionist show of 1879, in which she showed *La Loge,* a painting that reflects her mature Impressionist style with its emphasis on light, color, and composition. Well received by the French critics, she became a part of the Parisian art scene, but she did not wholly cut her ties with America; she exhibited at the Pennsylvania Academy of Fine Arts Annual in 1876 and again in 1878 and 1879. In 1878 she also had a painting in the Annual Exhibition of the National Academy of Design in New York. It is believed that these canvases were the first Impressionist paintings to be shown in America.

From then on, Mary Cassatt's career as a leading Impressionist was firmly established. In 1891 she had her first one-man show at the famous Parisian dealer Durand-Ruel, who had also shown Berthe Morisot, and her work was exhibited in London, New York, and Boston. Although her style remained basically Impressionist, her later work was very much influenced by Japanese prints. A large exhibition of Japanese wood blocks was shown in Paris in 1890. Mary Cassatt, who visited the show with Degas, was profoundly impressed by the prints, and their influence is apparent in her own graphic art, a field in which many critics feel she did her best work. Her later paintings are also influenced by Japanese art, especially in the clear outlines and the strong emphasis on color patterns.

By 1892 Mary Cassatt's reputation was so great, not only in France but also in her native country, that she was commissioned to do a mural for the Women's Building at the Chicago World's Columbian Exposition. The large scale of a wall painting was not suited to her style, but the very fact that she was asked to do it indicates the prestige she enjoyed. In the same year she bought a small château at Mesnil-Théribus called Beaufresne, which she paid for with money she had earned from her own work. It was here that she lived for the rest of her life and where she painted some of her finest pictures. Unlike Berthe Morisot, who had died when Impressionism was at the height of its success, Mary Cassatt lived well into the twentieth century, dying in 1926 at the age of eighty-two. Like many other artists who had been pioneers in their youth, she did not change with the times, and, as a result, she neither liked nor understood the modern movement. In her later years she was isolated and bitter, and at the end she was "very nearly blind, and querulous and vindictive."[25] She had no use even for Monet's late water lilies, which she said looked like glorified wallpaper, and she was contemptuous of Gertrude and Leo Stein, whom she accused of sensationalism. As Frederick Sweet relates in his excellent biography of Mary Cassatt, when she was taken by Mrs. Sears, a friend, to visit the Steins for one of their open houses in 1908, the friend took the precaution of having "her car and chauffeur wait outside the door, not knowing how the evening would go off. Mary Cassatt was introduced to a number of people, looked about

[25]F. Sweet, *Miss Mary Cassatt* (Norman, Oklahoma, 1966), p. 195.

Portrait of a Young Girl, by Mary Cassatt, 19th century. *Metropolitan Museum of Art, New York*

The Boating Party, by Mary Cassatt. *National Gallery, Washington, D.C.*

her at the dozens of early Picassos and Matisses, and finally went up to Mrs. Sears and said, 'I have never in my life seen so many dreadful paintings in one place; I have never seen so many dreadful people gathered together and I want to be taken home at once.' " But by that time Mary Cassatt had made her contribution to art, and as the Philadelphia *Inquirer* said in her obituary, she was "considered by the critics of two continents one of the best women painters of all time."

In the United States as in Europe, many women painters were the daughters or wives of artists. A notable example is Jane Stuart (ca. 1812–1888), the daughter of Gilbert Stuart, the portrait painter. Although she mostly copied her father's work, she also did some narrative paintings in a more personal style. The most remarkable women painters of that period were the Peale sisters of Philadelphia, whose grandfather had established the Pennsylvania Academy of Art and whose father, James, was also a well-known artist. Sarah Peale (1800–1885), the youngest of the three, became the first full-time professional woman painter in America and in 1824 was elected a member of the Pennsylvania Academy of Art. Working in Philadelphia, Baltimore, and Saint Louis, she was famous as a portrait painter and painted such eminent men as

Still Life with Watermelon, by Margaretta Peale, 19th century. *Smith College Museum of Art*

Lafayette and Daniel Webster. In her old age, she turned largely to still lifes, a form in which she and her sisters did some of their best work. These pictures, executed in a very plain, direct style, combine a good sense of composition with a strong feeling for the object. Her eldest sister, Anna Peale (1791–1878), was well known as a miniaturist and accompanied her father and uncle on their travels across the country. The other sister, Margaretta (1795–1882), excelled in painting fruits, although she also did portraits. All three had been encouraged in their career by their uncle, Charles Willson Peale, who believed in the equality and education of women.

Another favorite subject of nineteenth-century American artists was genre painting, and there was at least one woman of note among the practitioners of this form. Much admired in her own day and widely reproduced in popular commercial lithographs, she was all but forgotten when the public lost interest in this kind of sentimental narrative painting. In recent years she has been rediscovered, and a splendid exhibition of her work, accompanied by an excellent catalogue, was organized by the National Collection of Fine Arts in 1973.[26] Her name is Lilly Martin Spencer and she lived from 1822 to 1902, although her best work was done during the middle years of the nineteenth century. Like her male contemporaries William Sidney Mount, Jerome Thompson, George Caleb Bingham, and Eastman Johnson, she believed that art should record everyday life, and, although she had several opportunities, she never went to Europe

[26]Robin Bolton-Smith, *Lilly Martin Spencer, The Joys of Sentiment* (Washington: Smithsonian Institution Press, 1973).

because she felt no need to see the old masters or to exhibit her work in the Paris Salons.

Although Lilly Martin was born in England of French parents, she was brought to the United States as a child and grew up in Marietta, Ohio, where her father had received an appointment as a teacher. Her bent for art became apparent when she was a young girl, and two local painters who had studied at the Pennsylvania Academy helped her in her work. Her father, who also had an inclination toward art, was very sympathetic to his daughter's career. Her first exhibition was held at the local Episcopal church when she was nineteen years old. In 1841 she moved to Cincinnati where she began to study art seriously with John Insco Williams and she soon developed into a highly accomplished portrait painter, as is evident in the self-portrait from this period that is now in the Ohio Historical Center in Columbus. It shows a handsome dark girl with a dreamy expression, and is rendered in the romantic style of the period. In 1844 she married Benjamin Rush Spencer and had thirteen children, eight of whom grew to maturity. Their marriage, which was very happy, was most remarkable, especially at that time, for her husband completely subordinated his life to her career, much of the time taking care of the house and the children rather than pursuing a profession of his own.

In 1848 they moved to New York so that she would have better opportunities to exhibit and sell her work, and in 1858 they went to Newark, New Jersey, which they felt would be cheaper and better for the children. Although she never enjoyed a great success either financially or critically, she proved a very popular painter with the general public. The reproductions after her work, produced by Goupil, Vibert and Company, sold widely, and her own canvases were shown and distributed through the Western Art Union and the Cosmopolitan Art Association, organizations that promoted art with the help of lotteries. Her favorite subjects were those taken from the world around her, often involving members of her immediate family. *Child with Toy, Grandpa's Prodigies, Peeling Onions, The Young Husband: First Marketing,* and *The Picnic on the Fourth of July, A Day to Be Remembered* are typical of her best work, whereas her more pretentious allegorical paintings are her least successful. Her later life, during which she and her family first moved to Highland, New York, and then back to New York City, proved disappointing, for the critical standards and the general taste in art had changed, and the public no longer admired the kind of painting she was doing. She died in New York in 1902, aged eighty, in poverty and already forgotten.

Though these artists had received professional training and worked as established painters, there were many others who were never formally trained but who nonetheless pursued their artistic inclinations. Especially popular was watercolor painting, which was part of the curriculum of the female seminaries of the nineteenth century and was also studied at home. Today, these amateur artists are usually called primitives and, as such, they have great appeal to modern critics and collectors. The best are certainly among America's most charming nineteenth-century artists, and today many an amateur painting, decorative design, or embroidery is displayed in our museums next to the more finished, pretentious canvases of the professional painters.

Among the so-called American Primitives, the best known and perhaps the most outstanding is Eunice Pinney (1770–1849). Born in Simsbury of an old Connecticut family, she was typical of many of these amateur artists. She lived and worked largely in Windsor, was married twice, and had several children. Apparently, she did not take

Bedspread, by Mary Breed, 18th century.
Metropolitan Museum of Art, New York

Mrs. Clarke, the York Magnet, by Eunice
Pinney, 19th century. *Collection of Abby
Aldrich Rockefeller Folk Art Collection,
Williamsburg, Virginia*

up painting until she was forty and had married for the second time. Although she
never mastered the kind of illusionism and accurate sense of perspective and modeling
so popular with professional artists, her work has a freshness and vigor that theirs often
lacks. Her pictorial compositions with their careful drawing and fine sense of pattern
have a naïve charm, a quality that they might not have had if she had received formal
training in an art academy.

<

Reading the Legend, by Lilly Martin Spencer, 19th century. *Smith College Museum of Art*

6 WOMEN PAINTERS OF THE TWENTIETH CENTURY

THE TWENTIETH century, with its new sense of freedom and equality, brought women artists opportunities for education and self-expression that they had not previously enjoyed. In contrast to earlier centuries, women painters came from a wide variety of social and economic backgrounds, ranging all the way from the poorest working class to the most affluent bourgeoisie. Art academies and art schools, once chiefly the province of men, now accepted large numbers of women, and college and university art departments attracted numerous female students. This development was not limited to western Europe and the United States but also made itself felt in Latin America and Asia where female painters for the first time began to assume a more important role.

Although no accurate figures exist on how many women painters there are today, there is no question that in recent decades the number has grown immensely. The mid-century census figures showed that in the United States alone no fewer than two million people listed their main occupation as that of artist. It seems likely that about half were women and then, of course, there were countless others who were part-time or amateur painters. Strangely enough, this dramatic growth in the number of women artists has not produced a corresponding increase in major female painters. In fact, none of the important movements like Fauvism, Cubism, Expressionism, Surrealism, Social Realism, or Abstract Expressionism had women members who made really significant contributions, and no single female painter of the twentieth century has achieved the fame that Elisabeth Vigée-Lebrun, Angelica Kauffmann, Rosa Bonheur,

Berthe Morisot, and Mary Cassatt enjoyed in their day. No doubt part of the explanation lies in the fact that, in earlier periods, women artists were more exceptional, and therefore more attention was paid to them, but it still seems strange that the number of outstanding women painters has not increased.

The first seven decades of the twentieth century have produced numerous gifted women painters, and, though none has proved the equal of Matisse or Picasso, many of them have made important contributions to the art of our time. With so many to choose from, any selection is bound to be both arbitrary and subjective, but an attempt has been made to pick those who are the most important and to show how women painters were active in all the leading countries and in all the major artistic schools and tendencies of the twentieth century.

Of the modern French women painters, the two most important are undoubtedly Suzanne Valadon and Marie Laurencin, both very much part of the School of Paris and closely associated with famous male artists of their time. Suzanne Valadon is perhaps best known for being the mother of Utrillo and for leading a colorful, bohemian life, but she was also an artist of real significance in her own right. Born in Limoges into a working-class family in 1867, she started her life as a trapeze-rider in a circus but, after breaking her thigh, she became an artist's model in Montmartre, posing for painters like Puvis de Chavannes, Renoir, and Degas. A young woman of great beauty and already a gifted draftsman, she became friendly with Degas and Toulouse-Lautrec who admired her powerful line drawings. In spite of having no formal training, at sixteen she already had some success with her work. It was during these years that she had an illegitimate child, Maurice Utrillo, and that she married a well-to-do businessman.

Suzanne Valadon's independent career as a modern artist, however, began only when she was forty and she had divorced her husband and begun to live with the young painter André Utter, whom she later married. Profoundly influenced by Van Gogh and Gauguin and working in a style close to the Fauves, notably Matisse, she evolved a bold style of her own that made her a part of the avant-garde movement. In 1909 she exhibited for the first time with her son Utrillo, and from then on she had an established place in the Parisian art scene. Painting colorful, decorative flower pieces and still lifes, powerful nudes and expressive portraits, Suzanne Valadon emerged as an artist of real stature. In 1920 she moved to the Château Saint Bernard in the Ain, which was purchased with Utrillo's earnings, and there she lived for most of the rest of her life with her husband and her son. Producing a large number of oil paintings, drawings, and prints, she gained increasing recognition and was widely shown both in France and abroad. In an issue of *L'Opinion,* Robert Rey wrote that she is a "great artist on the same level as Berthe Morisot," and in his little volume on Valadon, Mermillon calls her "the foremost woman-artist of her time . . . one of our great, intuitively creative artists, to whom French painting owes its permanent youth."[27] While we may not agree completely with these opinions, Suzanne Valadon is certainly one of the significant women painters of the twentieth century, and she enjoys an even greater reputation today than she did at the time of her death in 1938.

Marie Laurencin, although working in Paris during many of the same years and associating with some of the same artists, was completely different from Suzanne Valadon. Born in Paris in 1885 into a middle-class family, she attended the Lycée

[27]M. Mermillon, *Suzanne Valadon* (Paris, 1950), Introduction.

Still Life—Lilacs and Peonies, by Suzanne Valadon, 20th century. *Metropolitan Museum of Art, New York*

Lamartine where she graduated in 1905 at an age when Suzanne Valadon already had a colorful career behind her. She studied at the Académie Humbert, a conventional art school which left her deeply dissatisfied but where she met Georges Braque who introduced her to the avant-garde art movements, first Fauvism and then Cubism. Through Braque she met Picasso, Matisse, Apollinaire, and Max Jacob, and became part of the circle meeting at the Steins and lived in the Montmartre district of Paris, although she never actually belonged to either the Fauves or Cubists. However, her early pictures, such as her self-portrait of 1906, now in the Museum of Modern Art in New York, and even more, her 1908 portrait of Picasso, reflect the influences of both these movements.

Marie Laurencin's own temperament, which was delicate and romantic, was not suited for this kind of revolutionary art and, as she matured and developed her own style, she turned into a poetic painter of great tenderness and lyricism. Critics have usually described her work as feminine, meaning that it is gentle and poetic rather than bold and expressive. Her favorite subjects were pale, slender young girls with doe eyes who often appear with children or graceful animals. If her pictures bear any resemblance to those of her male associates, they are most similar to Picasso's Rose

Creoles, by Marie Laurencin, 20th century. *Museum of Fine Arts, Boston*

Head of Woman, by Marie Laurencin, 20th century. *Findlay Gallery, New York*

Period works with their fragile, melancholy beauty. Her artist friends called her the muse, and she does indeed seem more like a lyric poet than a modern painter. Her favorite colors were delicate blues, pinks, grays, and subdued blacks rather than the brilliant colors of the Fauvists. Her forms were attenuated and graceful in contrast to the geometric forms of the Cubists, and yet her work in its simplification and distortion clearly reflects the influence of the modern movements. Her most successful years were in the 1920s, a decade that was congenial to the charm and grace of her painting. She continued to work in the same manner for the rest of her life, dying at age seventy in 1956. Her critical acclaim declined in her later years, although her popular appeal continued undiminished. One-man shows of her work were held in Paris and New York, and her work is represented in many leading museums and private collections.

A third woman artist who was associated with the avant-garde movement in Paris during the early years of the century was Sonia Delaunay. Born Sonia Terk in the Ukraine in 1885, she grew up in Saint Petersburg in the well-to-do bourgeois family of an uncle who had adopted her. In 1903 she went to Germany where she studied drawing in Karlsruhe, and in 1905, aged twenty, she arrived in Paris, which was to become her home. Although she was impressed by Van Gogh, Gauguin, and the Fauves, the most decisive influence on her art was Robert Delaunay, whom she married in 1910. Under his tutelage, she took up abstract painting and produced some of the most beautiful and revolutionary pictures of the years immediately preceding the First World War. The term Orphism is usually applied to the kind of work which she and her husband painted to distinguish its use of light and pure color from the more subdued palette of the Cubists.

During the 1920s Sonia Delaunay devoted herself primarily to decorative art, especially textiles and book designs in which she employed the principles of Cubism and Neo-Plasticism. In the mid-thirties she returned to painting, assuming a leading role along with her husband in the Abstract art movement. She painted a large mural for the 1937 Paris International Exhibition, for which she won a gold medal. However, it was not until the death of her husband in 1941 that Sonia Delaunay emerged as a major figure in her own right, and during the fifties and sixties, when she was already an old woman, her textile designs and her paintings achieved international recognition. An exhibition of her work and that of her husband was held in Bordeaux in 1959, in Turin in 1960, and in the Museum of Modern Art in Paris in 1964. The first important exhibition of her work was shown in Canada in 1965, a large retrospective was held in Paris in 1967, and a major book on her art, published in Paris and London, for the first time properly assesses her contributions to twentieth-century art.

Next to France, Germany was the most important center in the evolution of modern art. The outstanding German woman painter of the twentieth century was Paula Modersohn-Becker, an immensely gifted artist who, had she not died prematurely at thirty-one, might have become a leading figure in modern art. Born in Dresden in 1876, she and her family moved to Bremen when she was twelve years old. She attended art school in London, then studied in Bremen in the Pedagogical Institute and, finally, in Berlin. In 1897, when she was twenty-one, she visited the artists' colony at Worpswede near Bremen, which was to become her home and where she married the painter Otto Modersohn in 1901. Her early pictures, although marked by considerable talent, were a rather conventional reflection of the Realistic and Impressionist tendencies of the day. They are largely representations of the landscape and people of Worpswede, a picturesque village in the moors of North Germany.

The greatest influence in her life, however, was not her association with the artists in Worpswede, who tended to be romantic landscape painters of no great distinction, but a visit to Paris in 1900 where she discovered the paintings of Cézanne. As she herself said in a letter to the wife of the poet Rilke, who was her closest friend, seeing those pictures was like a thunderstorm, a great event that totally changed her outlook. Cézanne's simplicity and strength confirmed her own aspirations and helped her to evolve a new style that made her an important pioneer of modern art in Germany. Several additional stays in Paris further strengthened her resolve and also introduced her to the work of Van Gogh and Gauguin, which profoundly influenced her painting. Inspired by these masters of the Post-Impressionist movement, she simplified her forms, strengthened her drawing, flattened out her space, and began to use bold, two-dimensional areas of brilliant color, creating some of the most powerful and expressive paintings to come out of Germany at that time. She worked in comparative isolation, far removed from the art centers where others were groping with the same problems. Only a few friends and farsighted critics realized that Paula Modersohn-Becker was an artist of rare gift and originality. The painter's journals and

Girl with Floral Wreath, by Paula Modersohn-Becker.
Gallery of 20th Century Art, Berlin

letters, which were published after her death, give a vivid account of her struggles and discoveries, and they form a moving document of modern art. After seven intense and productive years, Paula Modersohn-Becker died in childbirth in 1907, leaving behind a rich artistic heritage that was not really appreciated until the next generation, when it was recognized as a vital contribution to modern German art.

The other outstanding German woman painter of the early twentieth century was Gabriele Münter. Born in Berlin in 1877, she studied in Munich and lived most of her life in the small Bavarian town of Murnau where she died in 1962 at the age of eighty-five. Unlike Paula Modersohn-Becker, who had little contact with other pioneers of modern German art, Gabriele Münter was intimately associated with the avant-garde artists of her time, notably Kandinsky and the painters of the Blue Rider group. Talking about those early years in an interview with Edouard Roditi in 1959, she said:

In 1901, I decided to move to Munich, but still found very little encouragement as an artist. German painters refused to believe that a woman could have real talent, and I was even denied access, as a student, to the Munich Academy. In those days, women could study art in Munich only privately, or in the studios of the Künsterinnenverein, the association of professional women artists. It is significant that the first Munich

Carpet with abstract figures, by Sophie Taüber-Arp. *Private collection, Zurich*

artist who took the trouble to encourage me was Kandinsky, himself no German but a recent arrival from Russia.[28]

Gabriele Münter was at the very center of the modern German movement. She lived with Kandinsky for a number of years, and they belonged to an art circle that included, in addition to the Russian Jawlensky and his companion Marianne de Werefkin, such famous artists as Klee, Marc, and Macke. She worked in a very modern style, using flat areas of bright colors and simplified forms. She was one of the founders of the New Artists Society of Munich and she was also one of the original members of the Blue Rider group, which was formed in 1911. Yet after settling in Murnau with Kandinsky in 1908, she became very interested in Bavarian peasant art, especially behind-the-glass painting, and she began using very simple forms and primitive images. The outbreak of the First World War, which forced Kandinsky to return to Russia, ended her association with this revolutionary artist and strengthened her tendency to go her own way, quite apart from the mainstream of modern art. After five years spent in Sweden and Denmark during the war and the immediate postwar years, the painter returned to Germany. From 1931 on, she lived in Murnau in semiretirement. Although her last years were far removed from the artistic and political turmoil of Munich and Berlin, for a brief period in her youth she was a vital force and influential figure in modern German art.

While Paula Modersohn-Becker and Gabriele Münter were associated with the early Expressionist movement, the Swiss-born Sophie Taüber-Arp was connected with

[28]E. Roditi, "Interview with Gabrielle Münter," *Arts Magazine* (January 1960), p. 39.

Dadaism and the Abstract movement. Born in Davos in 1889, Sophie Taüber studied in Saint Gall, Munich, and Hamburg from 1909 to 1912, and in 1916, at the age of twenty-seven, she became a teacher at the Zurich School of Industrial Arts, where she taught textile design until 1929. While in Zurich she became part of the Dada group, which had gathered in this neutral city to escape the insanity of the First World War. A revolutionary art movement dedicated to a nihilistic view of society, Dadaism gave poignant expression to the despair and meaninglessness of those bitter years that killed off the best of Europe's youth, including young artists like Marc and Macke. Sophie Taüber's own contribution to Dadaism consisted of a group of highly original mechanical puppets, abstract sculptures, and geometric constructions.

More important was her contribution to abstract art, for in 1916 she began painting nonfigurative geometric pictures and designing abstract textiles of great beauty. In 1926 she married the sculptor Jean Arp, who had also been associated with the Dadaists and the Abstract movement, and she settled with him in Meudon near Paris where she lived from 1928 until 1940, when the Nazis occupied the town. While in France, she was an active member of the Circle et Carré in 1930 and the Abstraction-Création group between 1931 and 1936. She was also a founder of the magazine *Plastique* and became an advocate of the Non-Objective school of abstract art, which used rigid geometric shapes and very formal compositions. During the war she moved to Grasse in southern France, and there she made some colored lithographs that are outstanding for their harmony of colors and clarity of forms. In 1943 she was killed in an accident while still at the height of her creativity.

Among the women painters in the United States, the best known and by far the most outstanding is Georgia O'Keeffe. In contrast to Mary Cassatt, the only other American woman artist who attained such eminence, her fame does not rest on work done in Europe virtually as a French artist, but is based wholly on her career in America. In fact, she only went to Europe in 1953 and 1954, when she was already sixty-six years old, and she was not particularly influenced by this experience. While the assessments of her achievement may differ, there is little doubt that she is a typically American and highly original painter who expressed her own sensibility, regardless of the major art movements in Europe.

Born in Sun Prairie, Wisconsin, in 1887, she spent her childhood on a large farm and has never lost her love for nature and the land, a love that is strongly expressed in her paintings. Her gifts were evident very early, and it is said that she decided to become an artist when she was ten years old. She went to high school in Madison, Wisconsin, and in Virginia, where her family moved in 1902, and from 1905 to 1908 she attended the Chicago Art Institute and the Art Students League in New York where she received a good academic training. After a stint of commercial art in Chicago, she had jobs teaching art in Amarillo, Texas, at Columbia College in South Carolina, and at the West Texas State Normal School. She also taught during summers at the University of Virginia. The formative influence of those years was studying with Arthur Dow at Teachers College, Columbia, in New York. He introduced her to modern and Oriental art and taught her to think of color and design as abstract elements expressing her own ideas and emotions.

Under the influence of Dow, Georgia O'Keeffe broke away from her academic background and developed into an extremely original and creative artist. It was her encounter with Alfred Stieglitz, the famous photographer and sponsor of the modern art movement in America, that enabled her to freely develop her gifts without any financial worries. Stieglitz, who at that time was running his celebrated 291 Gallery in New York, first saw her abstract drawings and watercolors in 1916, at once recognized her talent, and gave her a one-man show in 1917 when she was thirty years old. In 1924, the two were married. From then on her career proceeded smoothly with almost yearly exhibitions at Stieglitz's gallery, often with other members of the Stieglitz circle, such as Charles Demuth, Marsden Hartley, and John Marin. She had a retrospective at the Brooklyn Museum in 1927, a major exhibition in Chicago in 1943, and a large show at the Museum of Modern Art in 1946, the first woman artist so honored.

During all these years she continued to produce a body of remarkable work, which has established her as one of the most important American painters of the twentieth century. Her most famous works are perhaps her large flowers, which in a haunting way combine abstraction with very precise realism, and may well have been influenced by the kind of abstract treatment of natural forms found in the work of contemporary photographers like Strand and Cunningham. Although she simplifies her forms and does away with surface detail to bring out underlying patterns, her work is always based on visual reality, whether it is forms of nature like the flowers, trees, and mountains of her beloved New Mexico, or architecture such as the adobe buildings of the Southwest or the skyscrapers of New York. In all her work, she gives expression to a very personal kind of visual sensitivity and creates art of lasting beauty.

While Georgia O'Keeffe always derived her forms from the real world, there were other women painters in America who worked in a completely nonobjective style. Notable among them is Irene Rice Pereira, who has emerged as a most interesting American abstractionist. Born in Boston in 1907, she went to New York at an early age and studied at the Art Students League from 1928 to 1931. After a year in Paris and Italy, she settled down permanently in New York and had her first one-man show in 1933. Her early work was semiabstract, using machine forms and other geometric elements. But in 1937 she evolved a completely abstract style. Emphasizing straight lines, flat surfaces, and textures, these paintings are purely geometric and reflect the kind of work that had been developed by members of the Bauhaus in Germany and the De Stijl group in Holland. However, in her later work Rice Pereira added to these geometric elements the dimension of space, which is often ambiguous and involves complexities of depth and light that she felt mirrored the findings of modern science. She also worked with new materials, such as using several layers of glass, painting on parchment, and experimenting with various kinds of surfaces. She died in Marbella, Spain, in 1971 at the age of sixty-four.

Another outstanding American who worked in an abstract idiom was Anne Ryan (1889–1954), whose remarkable contribution has been fully recognized only in recent years, long after her death. Her artistic career was both brief and unusual. An Irish Catholic girl who was born in Hoboken, New Jersey, she attended a local convent school and Saint Elizabeth's College, made a conventional marriage to a lawyer in Newark, had two children, and began to write poetry, a volume of which was published in 1925. She took up painting with the encouragement of her friend Hans Hofmann in 1938 when she was almost fifty. Her first one-man show, which consisted of oils, was held in 1941 when she was fifty-two, and at the same time she took up graphic art under Hayter and made designs for ballet costumes and stage backdrops. But she only found her true form of expression when she saw a show of collages by Kurt Schwitters at the Rose Fried Gallery in 1948. Overwhelmed by their beauty, Anne Ryan, although she was already fifty-eight, at once began to make collages herself and, in the few years of life

A HISTORY OF WOMEN ARTISTS

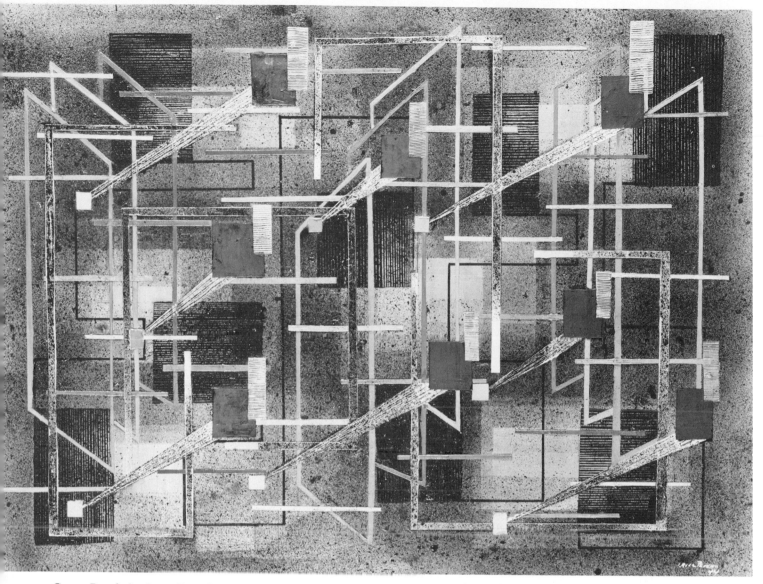

Green Depth, by Irene Rice Pereira, 20th century. *Metropolitan Museum of Art, New York*

left to her, produced some of the finest and most sensitive works in this medium to come out of America. Exhibitions of her collages at the Betty Parsons Gallery and in the 1951 "Abstract Painting and Sculpture in America" show at the Museum of Modern Art brought her work to the attention of the public. At the time of her death in 1954, at sixty-four, she was recognized as an artist of rare gifts, but it was not until 1974, at the Brooklyn Museum, that her collages received the kind of major exhibition they deserved.[29]

A very different artist is Doris Lee, whose work is devoted to the American scene. She was born in the small Illinois town of Aledo in 1905, and her paintings express her feeling for the landscape and the life with which she grew up. In spite of extensive travels in France and Italy and study under André Lhote in Paris, she continued to draw

[29]Catalogue by S. Faunce, *Anne Ryan Collages,* Brooklyn Museum, 1974.

The White Flower, by Georgia O'Keeffe,
20th century. *Whitney Museum of
American Art, New York*

The Seamstresses, by Doris Lee, 20th century. *Collection of the artist*

upon her roots in Midwestern America. Her mature work of the 1930s and '40s is marked by a sophisticated naïveté. Deeply influenced by the so-called primitive painting of nineteenth-century America, she combines this tradition with the formal awareness characteristic of modern art. Although she is very much part of the contemporary art scene, living in the Catskill art colony of Woodstock where she married Arnold Blanch, the painter who had been her teacher in San Francisco, she has preserved a certain innocence that gives her work its peculiar charm. She first came to national attention in 1936 with her mural *Rural Post Delivery,* which she painted for the new Post Office building in Washington, and with the picture *Thanksgiving Dinner,* which won the Logan award from the Art Institute of Chicago. In addition to her paintings, she has made numerous prints and illustrations, all in the rather whimsical primitive style for which she has become famous. Though she is no great innovator, Doris Lee is a delightful contemporary American woman painter.

In American painting of the second half of the century, at least two women artists, Joan Mitchell and Helen Frankenthaler, stand out as gifted and important painters. Both of them belong to what is usually called the second generation School of New York painters who work in the Abstract Expressionist style developed by men like Gorky, Pollock, and De Kooning. In spite of being deeply indebted to these older painters, both women developed their own style and have produced works that can stand up to any painting by their male contemporaries. Both come from comfortable backgrounds—Joan Mitchell's father was a doctor and Helen Frankenthaler's, a judge. They were encouraged to follow artistic careers, attended the best private women's colleges where they majored in art, and then continued their studies at outstanding art schools, supplemented by extensive stays abroad to familiarize themselves with the European art scene.

Joan Mitchell, who is the older of the two, was born in Chicago in 1926 and attended Smith College and the Art Institute of Chicago. After finishing her formal education, she spent two years in Europe where she came under the influence of modern French painting, notably by Cézanne, Van Gogh, Matisse, and Kandinsky. But she did not find her true form of expression until she went to New York, where she lived from 1950 to 1955, and discovered the work of Gorky and De Kooning. As she said later, it was seeing Franz Kline's black and white paintings on a brick wall that "blew her mind." Other important influences were Orozco, whose work she saw in Mexico, and above all Matisse, who she feels is the greatest painter of all. In light of this, it is interesting to note that she has lived in Paris since 1955.

Absorbing these various influences into a distinctive style of her own, Joan Mitchell emerged during the middle fifties as one of the significant younger American painters. Her large abstract canvases, beautifully executed and using color in a very painterly way, are among the finest paintings of our period. As Marcia Tucker says in the introduction to her excellent catalogue of the artist's large exhibition at the Whitney Museum in 1974:

> Her substantial reputation is based on the fact that her work, brilliantly conceived, flawlessly executed, shows us the extent to which a tradition can be made viable by excellence. Although Mitchell is no longer an Abstract Expressionist, the basic thrust and intent of her paintings are the same now as they were then. What is expressed by her work are the primal forms found in the natural world which provide us with the metaphors for our own existence.[30]

Even more important as a contemporary influence is Helen Frankenthaler. Born in New York City in 1928, she went to the Dalton School, where she studied with the Mexican painter Tamayo, and then to Bennington College where her teacher was Paul Feeley, who exposed her to the Cubist aesthetic. Her great revelation came when Clement Greenberg introduced her to the work of Gorky and, above all, Pollock who, with Kandinsky, has been the most important influence on her work. Her first one-man show was held in 1951 at the Tibor de Nagy Gallery, but it was not until 1953 that she broke away from the Cubist conventions of her early work and developed a freer, much more original style. Although at that point only twenty-five years old, Helen

[30]M. Tucker, *Joan Mitchell,* Whitney Museum, New York, 1974.

Frankenthaler had established herself as a major young painter of the New York School. Prominent painters like Kenneth Noland and Morris Louis, who visited her studio in 1953, were much impressed with her work and have acknowledged their debt to her,[31] and Frank O'Hara of the Museum of Modern Art praised her work. Numerous one-man shows followed, and individual works were included in important group shows, notably the exhibition of "Artists of the New York School, Second Generation," at the Jewish Museum, and "Young America 1957—thirty American Painters and Sculptors under thirty-five"—at the Whitney Museum of American Art. In the following year she married the painter Robert Motherwell and spent some time in France and Spain, where she had already traveled extensively during previous summers. In 1966 she was one of four Americans chosen for the American representation at the Venice Biennale, and in 1969, at the age of forty, she was given a retrospective at the Whitney Museum that was cosponsored by the International Council of the New York Museum of Modern Art and was also shown in London, Hanover, and Berlin.

In contrast to the tortured paintings of Gorky and Pollock, Helen Frankenthaler's work is poetic in character, using freely flowing forms and lyrical color. Although she has denied any Oriental influence, it has some of the spontaneity of Zen painting and Japanese calligraphy. As she said in an interview, "One hopes every picture will be a new birth, a fresh experience within a growing framework." Using large surfaces and letting the canvas show through, she employs colors and forms in a sensitive yet powerful way, combining the spirit of Abstract Expressionism with a delicacy and subtlety not found in the work of male painters of her generation. This is particularly true of the pictures from the fifties that many critics regard as her finest paintings. In more recent years she has tended to use large forms and flat areas of pure colors, probably reflecting the more recent tendencies in New York School painting. Yet she does so not as an imitator but as an extremely individual artist who has developed her own style.

The great change in the position of women is even more strikingly illustrated in Latin America and Asia, where for the first time important female painters have emerged. In fact, the three outstanding women artists of South America—Maria Helena Vieira da Silva, who is of Brazilian stock; Leonor Fini, who was born in Argentina; and Marisol, who came from Venezuela—are much better known internationally than any of their male colleagues. Only the Mexican muralists enjoy an equal reputation. Yet it must be said that all three had to leave their tradition-bound societies in order to fully develop their artistic potential and pursue careers as creative artists.

Maria Helena Vieira da Silva was born in 1908 in Lisbon of Brazilian parents. She studied sculpture under Bourdelle and Despiau in Paris in 1928, but she soon turned to painting and became a pupil of Léger, Friesz, and Bissière. Her most influential work, however, was done under Stanley William Hayter in his famous Atelier 17. In 1930 she married the Hungarian painter Arpad Szenés, who has been a great support in her work. At the outbreak of the Second World War she first went to Lisbon and then spent 1940 to 1947 in Rio de Janeiro. It was during these years that her work was exhibited in the Brazilian section of the Unesco show of 1946. However, in 1947 she returned to France and today is considered a member of the École de Paris. By the 1950s she had become internationally famous, exhibiting not only in Paris and New York but in many

---

[31] B. Rose, *Helen Frankenthaler* (New York, 1970), p. 14.

Svengali, by Helen Frankenthaler, 20th century. *Collection of John and Kimiko Powers, New Jersey*

other cities, such as London, Lisbon, Stockholm, Basel, and Hanover. In 1966, she won the Grand Prix National des Arts, the highest award that the French government can give an artist.

The titles she gives her pictures suggest the strange fascination and mystery of her work, which combines elements of cubism with elements derived from surrealism. To give some examples, a picture of 1947 is called *Enigme,* one of 1950 is *Nocturne,* and others from the fifties are *Perspectives Urbaniques, Les Grandes Constructions,* and *Le Part Illuminé.* Working with complex linear forms suspended in space, she creates a strange and haunting world for, as she once said, "when I make a painting, I always forget what I may have seen." Her images, however, are clearly derived from architectural forms. For example, the impressions she absorbed on a visit to New York in 1961 are reflected in her work of the sixties. In his introduction to the catalogue of her show at the Knoedler Gallery, John Rewald characterizes her art in a very perceptive way. He says:

> There are incredible depths in her paintings and impenetrable spaces, shifting planes, delicate colors, and mysterious horizons, all empty, innocent of occupants, yet vibrant with shimmering light. There are vistas that exist nowhere but have become real because Vieira da Silva has brought them into being; they are the spirits of her journeys into those distant spheres which nourish her imagination.[32]

Leonor Fini was born in Buenos Aires in 1908, the same year as Vieira da Silva. Her father was an Argentine and her mother an Italian from Trieste. The young artist began her career in Italy where she came under the influence of Carra, a prominent member of the Pittura Metafisica school. She exhibited in Milan, but in 1933 she moved to Paris. This was the time of Picasso's Rose Period pictures with their graceful figures and melancholy sentiment, and they impressed her most and had a lasting influence on her work. She was also associated with the Paris Surrealists of the 1930s, although she never formally became a member of their group. It was during these years that her art first aroused attention and this led to the inclusion of her work in the exhibition called "Fantastic Art, Dada, and Surrealist Art" held at the Museum of Modern Art in New York in 1936. During the postwar period, her reputation has steadily risen. An exhibition in Paris in 1945 was followed by others in Rome, Brussels, and New York, and today she is by far the best-known and the outstanding female painter of the Surrealist school.

An artist of great technical mastery in spite of being self-taught, Leonor Fini combines a meticulously objective style with a strange subject matter derived from the world of the subconscious. This fantastic and often surrealistic quality gives her work a weird fascination and yet at the same time makes it repelling and upsetting. It has a strong erotic element, often of a frankly lesbian character, with slender graceful girls reaching out for each other or making love. It is not by pure chance that she illustrated the Marquis de Sade's *Juliette* and Genet's La Galière, for her world, too, is one of unconventional sexual behavior and bizarre eroticism. Her more recent work is perhaps best characterized as Magic Realism. It represents beautiful, elegant young girls and genre scenes painted with great precision and clarity. This tendency is especially

[32]J. Rewald, *Vieira da Silva,* Catalogue of Exhibition at Knoedler Gallery, New York, 1971.

The Tree, by Maria Helena Vieira da Silva, 20th century. *Vassar College Art Gallery*

marked in her paintings of the 1960s in which some of the ambiguity and strangeness of her earlier work give way to more conventional imagery.

In Asia women had been active in crafts but had had little opportunity to be trained as painters. It was thus a revolutionary innovation when, in Tokyo in 1876, upon opening the first Western-style art school, there were six females in the first class. The result of this development, as well as the generally more liberal attitude toward women in modern Japan, was that by the twentieth century a number of Japan's best-known painters were women. Outstanding among those working in the Japanese style was Uemura Shoen (1875–1949), who specialized in traditional Japanese subjects rendered in a romantic style based on Ukiyo-e prints. Far more numerous, however, were the women artists working in a Western style. Migishi Setsuko, who was born in 1905 and spent several years in Paris, excelled in abstract still-life and flower paintings in the style of Braque. Katsura Yukiko, born in 1913, painted highly individual pictures in a surrealistic style and produced sensitive collages using Japanese rice paper, and Tanaka Atsuko, born in 1932, was a leading abstract painter of her generation.

Among Chinese women painters, the most interesting contemporary artist is Tseng Yu-ho, who was born in Peking in 1923 and was trained in traditional Chinese painting.

Painters of the Twentieth Century   81

第六回現代日本美術展
主催 毎日新聞社出品

作

品

桂ユキ子

A Tiger, by Katsura Yukiko, 20th
century. *Collection of the artist*

However, after being exposed to modern Western art and settling in Hawaii, she
developed a style that combines traditional Chinese materials and techniques with
contemporary artistic forms and ideas. The result is an art that preserves much of the
Chinese sensibility and yet is wholly modern in spirit. The same fusion of East and
West is found in the pictures of India's greatest modern woman painter, Amrita
Sher-Gill (1913–1941). Influenced by the work of Cézanne and Gauguin, which she
encountered in Paris, her paintings combine elements of modern Western art with
Indian subject matter and a vivid feeling for Indian life.

Away and Over, by Tseng Yu-ho, 20th century. *Collection of the artist*

Bride's Toilet, by Amrita Sher-Gill, 20th century. *Private collection, Bombay*

7 WOMEN SCULPTORS FROM MEDIEVAL TO MODERN TIMES

THE GREATEST resistance to women artists was in the field of sculpture. In Neolithic times and in all primitive civilizations with which we are familiar, sculpture was the prerogative of the men of the society. No doubt one of the reasons for this was purely physical, since it was assumed that the female sex, being weaker, was not suited for the hard manual labor required in carving stone, chopping wood, or working in metal, a view still prevalent in the nineteenth century and even found today, long after women have demonstrated their abilities in this field. However, another reason, especially in primitive societies, is that sculpture was connected with the magic and religious aspects of social life and was therefore considered a more significant art form and restricted to the male sex. It was probably for these reasons that there were practically no women sculptors during antiquity. Even in ancient Greece, which had women painters, there is no record of women doing any stone carvings or bronze images, the one exception being the potter's daughter who is supposed to have invented relief sculpture, but this is undoubtedly a legend and it in no way suggests that the girl was actively employed as a professional sculptor.

The first woman sculptor of any significance of whom there is a record is Sabina von Steinbach, the daughter of Erwin von Steinbach, the master carver responsible for the sculptural decorations of the Cathedral of Strassburg, a masterpiece of Gothic architecture. Tradition has it that the best of these thirteenth-century stone carvings, notably those on the portal of the southern aisle, were executed by Sabina. Of these

Church and Synagogue, by Sabina von Steinbach. *Strassburg Cathedral*

figures, those representing the Christian Church and the Jewish tradition have always been considered as among the finest sculptures at Strassburg and among the supreme creations of German medieval art. Certainly, the grace and beauty of these delicately carved female figures represent a high point in the history of Gothic sculpture.

There are two reasons for believing that these works were actually done by Sabina von Steinbach. First and most telling, a scroll held by the figure of the Apostle John has inscribed on it in Latin, "The Grace of God be with thee, O Sabina, Whose hands from this hard stone have formed my image." The second piece of evidence is an old painting at Strassburg which shows the youthful sculptor kneeling at the foot of the archbishop in order to receive from him his blessing and a wreath of laurel, which he is placing on her brow. "This painting attests the popular belief in the tradition that Sabina, after seeing her statues deposited in their niches, was met by a procession of priests who came, with the prelate at their head, for the purpose of conferring this honor upon her."[33]

The only prominent woman sculptor of the Renaissance was Properzia di Rossi, who was mentioned by Vasari and enjoyed a considerable reputation during her lifetime. She was a native of Bologna, as were many of the outstanding female painters

[33] Ellet, *Women Artists,* p. 31.

of the Renaissance. She was probably born in 1490 or 1491 and died in 1530. According to Vasari, as well as other contemporary reporters, she was a great beauty and an accomplished musician as well as an artist, and so well educated that "in many scientific studies she gained distinction well calculated to awaken the envy not only of most women but also of men." Her first work consisted of minute carvings in peach stones, which were much admired. One of them is said to have presented Christ's Crucifixion, showing not only Christ himself but numerous tiny figures representing the executioners, disciples, women, and soldiers. However, she soon turned to large-scale sculptures executed in marble, and it is for these that she is famous. Among them are a bust of Count Alessandro de Pepoli in Bologna, a characteristic example of Italian Renaissance portrait sculpture, and a relief carving in the Church of San Petronio in Bologna, which represents Potifar's wife seeking to detain Joseph by holding his garment. Vasari calls it "a lovely picture sculptured with womanly grace, and more than admirable." He also says that the figure of the woman is a self-portrait of the artist. It is certainly not a very original work, for it follows the style of Jacopo della Quercia, who had worked at the same church, and it is ultimately derived from the artistic tradition established by Donatello. However, it does indicate that Renaissance women, given the opportunity, were able to do creditable works of sculpture.

The situation for women sculptors was not much better during the seventeenth and eighteenth centuries, and only a few female artists were actively engaged in sculpture. During the Baroque period, the best known was a Spanish artist, Louisa Roldan, who was the daughter of the well-known sculptor Pedro Roldan. Born in Seville in 1656 and dying in Madrid in 1704, she was a contemporary of several Spanish women painters who were also active at the Spanish capital. Her work consists largely of wooden and clay figures, some of which are still extant. Her best known sculpture is a statue of Saint Michael that she made for the Escorial, but more characteristic are numerous small carvings of the Virgin and Adoration of the Shepherds groups which were admired for their delicacy and grace. Charles II of Spain was a special patron of hers and appointed her to the post of sculptor in ordinary to the king.

Of the female sculptors working during the eighteenth century, the best known was the English Anne Seymour Damer, who was probably more remarkable as a person than as an artist, but who did enjoy considerable fame in her lifetime. Born in 1748, the daughter of Field Marshal Henry Seymour Conway and Caroline Campbell, whose father was the Duke of Argyle, she grew up in the world of the aristocracy. Her cousin, Horace Walpole, contributed to her education, and the philosopher David Hume, who was one of her friends, is said to have encouraged her to become a sculptor. She was trained in working in marble by John Bacon, a British sculptor, and by the Italian artist Giuseppe Ceracchi, who at that time was working in England and who made a portrait statue of his pupil, which is now in the British Museum. She had a brief, unhappy marriage to John Damer, which ended in his suicide. After her husband's death, she traveled in France, Italy, and Spain, studying sculpture and continuing her creative work. Famous men like Nelson sat for her, Napoleon granted her an interview, and when Walpole died, he left her his celebrated Gothic-style villa at Strawberry Hill with its rich art collection and large library to be enjoyed during her life. An emancipated woman and a champion of liberty, she sided with the American revolutionaries and took an active interest in political affairs. She died at the age of eighty in 1828.

As an artist, Anne Damer was a neoclassicist who worked in clay, plaster of Paris,

>

Joseph and Potifar's Wife, by Properzia di Rossi, 16th century. *Church of San Petronio, Bologna*

marble, and bronze, and produced a large body of work that was much admired in its day. Horace Walpole said:

> Mrs. Damer's busts from life are not inferior to the antique. Her shock dog, large as life, and only not alive, has a looseness and softness in the curls that seemed impossible in terra cotta; it rivals the marble one of Bernini in the royal collection. The ancients have left us but five animals of equal merit ... the talent of Mrs. Damer must appear in the most distinguished light.[34]

Modern critics have been less enthusiastic in their assessment of her work. Professor Chandler Post in his history of sculpture refers to her works "as pieces of statuary of quite secondary value" and even hints that sometimes her masters applied the finishing touches. In his opinion, she was a person who took art as an elegant pastime. Her best works were her portrait busts, such as that of Sir Joseph Banks, now in the British Museum, and her statue of George II in the Register Office in Edinburgh, while her larger allegorical pieces have little appeal for modern taste.

Although there were many more women sculptors in the nineteenth century, no important figure stands out. In France the best was Félicie de Fauveau who, although born in 1802 in Italy, was taken to Paris as an infant and grew up in the French capital. Although she received little formal training, she was able to develop her gifts on her own, and she enjoyed the encouragement and friendship of such distinguished contemporaries as Baron Gros, Delaroche, Giraud, and Ary Scheffer. A romantic and a passionate Royalist, she had an extremely successful career under the Bourbons, particularly Charles X, who gave her a small pension and honored her with a gold medal for the work she exhibited at the Exposition des Beaux-Arts. After the revolution of 1830 she fled Paris and joined the Royalist forces in the Vendée, where she was known as the Heroine of the Vendée. Captured and put in prison for eight months, she escaped from France and in 1834 settled in Florence, where she spent the remainder of her life. She died in 1886.

Félicie de Fauveau's work was romantic in style and reflected her love of the medieval period. Using various materials—marble, wood, bronze, gold, silver, steel, and iron—she produced a large body of work which was eagerly collected, so that examples may be seen not only in France and Italy but in England and Russia as well. The first major work she exhibited was a group from Sir Walter Scott's novel, *The Abbot,* and a portrait of Queen Christina of Sweden, subjects that indicate her romantic temperament. Characteristic of her interest in Christian rather than classical subject matter was her bronze statue of Saint George and her Martyrdom of Saint Dorothea which she showed at the Paris World Exposition of 1855. Among her most important works in Italy is the funeral monument of a seventeen-year-old girl, which she did for the Church of Santa Croce in Florence. She also made the tomb for her friend Baron Gros, the romantic painter, which shows him with Saint Geneviève and which is now in the museum at Toulouse. In addition to large works, she designed weapons, jewelry, and decorative objects.

The United States produced its first women sculptors during the nineteenth century. The center of their activity was Rome, where, beginning around 1850, a number of American sculptors, both male and female, had settled. In the introduction to an

[34]Ellet, *Women Artists*, p. 175.

> Tomb of Louise Favreau, by Félicie de Fauveau, 19th century. *Church of Santa Croce, Florence*

interesting exhibition of the work of these early American women sculptors, held at the Vassar College art gallery in 1972, William Gerdts says:

> Life was congenial for our sculptors there. Some were more active in the general social life of the period than others, but they stayed, for the most part, within the framework of the Anglo-American colony, with numerous dinner parties, amateur theatricals, balls and the like. Visits from prospective patrons was very much part of the weekly activities and guidebooks were published in Rome, describing not only the sculptors and painters whose studios could be found on such and such a street, but what works might be seen in each and which were the latest conceptions upon which the artists were working. Patronage naturally followed, to some extent, a nationalistic course, with Americans on the Grand Tour visiting the studios of their fellow nationals, ordering an ideal piece or having their portraits modelled, and then returning home to await the delivery of their orders, many months or even years later.[35]

Among those located in Rome were Harriet Hosmer, Florence Freeman, Margaret Foley, and Edmonia Lewis. The best known and most successful was Harriet Hosmer, a native of Watertown, Massachusetts (1820–1908). She arrived in Rome in 1852 and became a pupil of the English sculptor John Gibson. While her work was neither very original nor outstanding, it certainly demonstrated that American women sculptors could hold their own with their male colleagues, and pieces such as her *Sleeping Faun* of 1865 and *Bust of Daphne* of 1854, now in Saint Louis, are competent examples of Neo-Classic sculpture. Her most ambitious work was a huge statue of Senator Benton. Born in the same year was her fellow New Englander Margaret Foley, a native of Dorset, Vermont (1820–1877). She arrived in Rome in 1860 and became famous for her portraits and her large marble relief medallions. Her most impressive work was a marble fountain, shown at the Philadelphia Centennial Exposition of 1876, and a bronze monument to Stonewall Jackson in Richmond.

It was only during the twentieth century that women sculptors emerged as major artists with positions equal to those of men. The first among these and one of the most famous female artists to work in any medium was Barbara Hepworth (1903–1975). Born in Wakefield, Yorkshire, in the north of England, the young artist was one of those fortunate people who knew what she wanted from the very start and received love and encouragement from all sides. Her father, an engineer, believed in giving his daughters the same educational opportunities as his sons, and the Wakefield Girls' High School encouraged her artistic development by getting her a fellowship at the Leeds School of Art and later at the Royal College of Art in South Kensington. She credits a lecture on Egyptian sculpture, which she heard when she was seven, with arousing her interest in the art. It was given by the headmistress of her school. Looking back on these early Yorkshire years, she said:

> The whole of this Yorkshire background means more to me as the years have passed. I draw on these early experiences not only visually in texture and contour, but humanly. The importance of man in landscape was stressed by the seeming contradiction of the industrial town springing out of the inner beauty of the country. This

[35]W. Gerdts, *The White Marmorean Flock, Nineteenth Century American Women Neo-classical Sculptors,* Vassar College, 1972.

Portrait of Woman, by Margaret Foley, 19th century. *Collection of Professor and Mrs. William Rhoads, New Paltz, New York.*

paradox expressed for me most forcibly the fundamental and ideal unity of man with nature which I consider to be one of the basic impulses of sculpture.[36]

Her student years were followed by a stay in Italy where she married a young English sculptor, John Skeaping, and became interested in ancient art. But the decisive influences on her work came from Henry Moore, whom she met at the Leeds School, and the modern abstract movement. In Paris she visited the studios of Brancusi and Mondrian. After her divorce from Skeaping, she became friends with, and later married, Ben Nicholson, the British abstract painter. Her first one-man show of 1928, when she was only twenty-five, was followed by numerous other exhibitions both in England and abroad. Certainly no other woman artist of the twentieth century has received such early and universal recognition, culminating in her winning the Grand Prix at the São Paulo Biennale in 1959, a major retrospective at the Tate Gallery in 1968, and a commission from the United Nations to design the memorial to its late secretary-general, Dag Hammarskjöld, in 1963. After her early years in London and repeated visits to the continent, in 1939 Barbara Hepworth and her husband moved to Saint Ives, Cornwall, where the sculptor acquired the Trewyn Studio in which she

[36] *Barbara Hepworth,* Tate Gallery Catalogue, London, 1968, p. 7.

Figure in a Landscape, by Barbara Hepworth, 20th century. *Smith College Museum of Art*

worked until her death, surrounded by her artist friends, children, and grandchildren.

Barbara Hepworth's work, like her life, was all of a piece, developing organically and culminating in the wonderful sculptures of her maturity. Abstract in form yet based on nature, her works fused natural shapes with the archetypal forms of prehistoric sculpture. Titles such as *Menhir, Ancestral Figures, Sea Forms, Waves, Hollow Oval Totem,* and *Talismen* suggest the world from which she derived her imagery. Recalling her early impressions of the landscape of her native region, she said:

> The hills were sculptures; the roads defined the form. Above all, there was the sensation of moving physically over the contours of fullnesses and concavities, through hollows and over peaks—feeling, touching, seeing, through mind and hand and eye. This sensation has never left me. I, the sculptor, am the landscape. I am the form and I am the hollow, the thrust and the contour.[37]

Like Arp and Moore, the two male sculptors who influenced her the most, Barbara Hepworth believed that the material itself should play an important role in the creation of the form, so that the texture and color of the material were essential ingredients in her sculpture. While the human figure was clearly recognizable in her early work, her forms became more and more abstract, taking on a life of their own derived from

[37]Barbara Hepworth, *Barbara Hepworth: A Pictorial Autobiography* (New York: Frederick A. Praeger, 1970), p. 9.

Dag Hammarskjöld Memorial, by Barbara Hepworth, 20th century. *United Nations, New York*

Praying Mantis, by Germaine Richier, 20th century. *Marlborough Gallery, New York*

nature but existing in a world of pure forms not unlike the Neolithic carvings at Stonehenge. Her titles—*Constructions* or *Two Forms*—suggested the kind of primeval images she was creating, images that transformed her impressions of the landscape into something like Plato's world of ideal shapes.

While Barbara Hepworth was the outstanding woman sculptor of the abstract school, the French artist Germaine Richier is the best female exponent of expressionistic sculpture. Born in Grans near Arles in Provence in 1904, she is a contemporary of Barbara Hepworth, but that is about the only thing they have in common. After studying at the École des Beaux-Arts in Montpellier from 1922 to 1925, Germaine Richier went to Paris where she became a student of Bourdelle. Her early work was classical in style and rather conventional. Her first show was held in Paris in 1934, when she was thirty years old. During the 1940s she did animal sculptures of a kind that foreshadowed the nature of her mature work, for the creatures she chose were spiders, owls, bats, and toads rendered in a grotesque style with elongated extremities and strangely distorted forms. In the postwar period Germaine Richier developed her mature style and began to enjoy considerable success not only in France but also abroad. Her work was included in the "New Images of Man" show at the Museum of Modern Art in New York, and a large retrospective of her work was held in Zurich in 1963. In 1959, when she was fifty-five years old, she died in Montpellier, where she had begun her career.

Although she came from Provence, the most classical section of France, Germaine Richier expressed the anguish and torment of life in forms that often shocked the public. Her *Crucified Christ* of 1950, created for the Church of Notre Dame de Grâce at Passy, created heated controversy, and her monstrous creatures with gangrenous limbs, obscene stomachs, and distorted anatomy are disquieting in the extreme. *The Ogre* of 1951, the grotesque *Bird Man* of 1955, and the *Tauromachia* of 1953 are weird creations of her morbid fantasy, filled with ambiguity and a strange haunting imagery, no doubt symbolizing the tortured soul of the artist and her time. It is not pure chance that when Germaine Richier, who was also a distinguished printmaker, illustrated a book in 1949, she chose Arthur Rimbaud's *Une Saison en Enfer* as the subject for her engravings.

It was in the United States, especially during the fifties and sixties, that women sculptors showed the greatest originality and creative power. Coming from many different backgrounds and working in many different styles, these artists demonstrated beyond doubt that women, given the opportunity to become sculptors, were capable of producing work as significant and rewarding as that of any of their male colleagues. While there had been a few accomplished sculptors in the United States during the nineteenth and the first half of the twentieth century, it was only in the period after the Second World War—when New York was rapidly becoming the art capital of the world—that major sculpture was produced in America. Some of the best of it was the work of women.

The oldest and by far the most outstanding is Louise Nevelson, who in the eyes of many critics is the most original female artist alive today and a great sculptor of the twentieth century. Born in 1899 in Kiev, Russia, she came from a Jewish family that emigrated to America in 1905. The young Louise Berliawsky grew up in Rockland, Maine. At an early age she was determined not only to be an artist but to work in sculpture since the three-dimensional form appealed to her. An early marriage to

Charles Nevelson ended in divorce because she felt hemmed in by her husband's family. She had one child, Myron Nevelson, who is now also a sculptor. Between 1928 and 1933, she studied at the Art Students League and under Hans Hofmann in Munich. For a time she also assisted Diego de Rivera with his murals, worked as a teacher at the Educational Alliance School of Art, and studied dance, which she has always loved and finds very congenial. However, for her the thirties were primarily years of learning and searching for her artistic identity. Nevertheless, Emily Genauer, in reviewing Nevelson's first works that were shown at the ACA Gallery said, "Louise Nevelson is the most interesting of the contest winners. . . . important are five wood sculptures, unlike anything you've ever seen before, wood sculpture conceived abstractly and with special concern for the tensions of planes and volumes." Her first one-man show was at the Nierendorf Gallery in 1941, and it brought her to the attention of the critics and the public. Several other individual and group exhibitions during the forties established Louise Nevelson's position as one of the most original American sculptors. Trips to Mexico to study Pre-Columbian art, which, along with African and North American Indian art, she had always admired, provided stimulus and inspiration. But it was not until the fifties, after her shows at the Grand Central Modern Gallery, whose director, Colette Roberts, was a great admirer of her work, that Louise Nevelson had the kind of major breakthrough she had been waiting for. Her 1955 show entitled "Ancient Games and Ancient Places," followed by "The Royal Voyage" of 1956, and culminating in her 1958 show called "Moon Garden + One" placed her in the forefront of contemporary American artists. Works were bought by the Whitney Museum, the Brooklyn Museum, and the Museum of Modern Art. Hilton Kramer, at that time the editor of *Arts Magazine,* wrote a long, laudatory review in which he said, "For myself, I think Mrs. Nevelson succeeds where the painters often fail."[38]

By 1959 Louise Nevelson, now a woman of sixty, had achieved the kind of recognition few artists ever attain. The Museum of Modern Art included her in the "Sixteen Americans" show of that year; she was invited to show in the United States Pavilion at the Venice Biennale of 1962; she was the first woman and the first sculptor to be asked to join the Sidney Janis Gallery, at that time the most prestigious in New York; she was elected president of National Artists Equity in 1965; and two years later she was given a large retrospective at the Whitney Museum. Books were written about her and, after the death of her friend David Smith, many critics spoke of her as the greatest living American sculptor. Her unconventional appearance with crazy hats and false eyelashes and her habit of smoking Tiparillos established her as an offbeat character who thoroughly enjoyed her role as an independent, rather eccentric, person. It is said that when a museum director, who had an appointment with her, apologized for being ten minutes late, she replied, "You are ten years late."

In speaking of creative art, Louise Nevelson once said, "I don't think an 'artist' has a right to that title until he finds a unique, a private way of making his statement."[39] This she has certainly done. While in the past even the greatest female artists were largely derivative, Louise Nevelson developed a unique style that bears no resemblance to that of any male artist of her time. As she herself said, "I have always wanted to show the

[38]H. Kramer, "The Sculpture of Louise Nevelson," *Arts Magazine* (June 1958), pp. 26–29.
[39]"Louise Nevelson," *Current Biography* (1967), pp. 314–17.

world that art is everywhere except that it has to pass through a creative mind."[40]

Her works have been called assemblages and have been compared to the Cubist constructions of Picasso, the Surrealist objects of Miró, and the Merzbau of Schwitters. Louise Nevelson would be the first to admit that she was influenced by Cubism, Surrealism, Constructivism, and Collage. She would also not deny that the magic power of African sculptures, which she collects and displays on her walls, the wild fantasy of American Indian art, and the majestic presence of Pre-Columbian art all stimulated and inspired her, but the fact is that she has absorbed all these influences and still created a distinctive art, which gives expression to the urban landscape and the unique aesthetic sensibility of our time.

Using all kinds of wooden objects, mostly discarded things like packing crates, broken pieces of furniture, and abandoned architectural ornaments, all of which she has hoarded for years, she assembles them into architectural constructions of great beauty and power. Gluing and nailing them together, painting them black (and in some later works white or, more rarely, gold) and placing them in boxes, she creates assemblages, walls, and entire environments that create a mysterious, almost awe-inspiring, atmosphere. Although she herself has denied any symbolic or religious intent and says that her creations simply express her feelings and ideas, the titles she gives these works, such as *Sky Cathedral* or *Night Cathedral,* suggest such connotations. Creating very freely with no sketches, but carefully assembling bits and pieces of wood, she constructs sculptures of great power and presence. In some ways, her most ambitious works are closer to architecture than to traditional sculpture, but then neither Louise Nevelson nor her art fits into any neat category.

The other outstanding American women sculptors belong to a younger generation and represent a very different aspect of contemporary art. Marisol and Niki de Saint Phalle, both born in 1930, might be considered part of Pop art while Lee Bontecou, who was born a year later, is one of the artists working in a field that has been called Assemblage. All three came into prominence during the sixties, received almost instant recognition, and were bought by major museums and collections, suggesting that the present situation is more open to young artists than it was in the past. Working in many different media and using very individual styles, they reflect the diversity and experimentation characteristic of present-day American art and which make New York the most vital and influential art center in the world today.

Interestingly enough, Marisol Escobar is not a native American but was born in Paris of Venezuelan parents. During most of the war she lived in Caracas but she moved to Los Angeles when she was a girl. At sixteen she decided to become a painter and she studied at the Jepson School in Los Angeles, at the École des Beaux-Arts in Paris, at the Art Students League in New York, and finally with Hans Hofmann from 1951 to 1954. As she herself said in summarizing her early work, "I painted like a Hofmann student." It was not until she turned to sculpture that she found her true calling. Interestingly enough, she was first inspired by South American folk carvings. In characterizing this phase of her development, she said, "It started as a kind of rebellion. Everything was so serious. . . . I started doing something funny so that I would be

[40]Ibid.

Royal Tide II, by Louise Nevelson, 20th century. *Whitney Museum of American Art, New York*

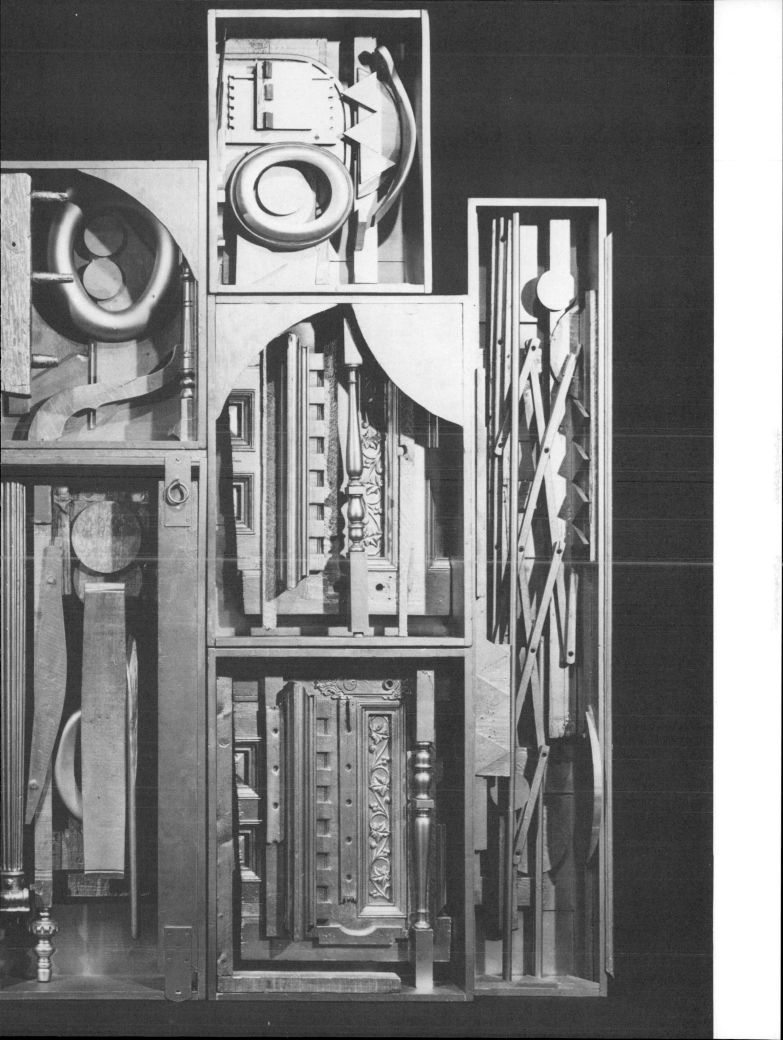

happier and it worked."[41] By 1958 she had developed her mature style which consisted of large wooden figures, often painted, especially in the faces and clothes, and using all sorts of other materials such as clay for the faces and paper, cloth, and photographs. Dorothy Miller, who included her in the show "Americans, 1963" at the Museum of Modern Art, called her work "a very individual sophisticated expression in a folk art idiom." It has been variously described as Neo-Dada, Pop, and New Realism, but Marisol sees it merely as an expression of herself. She also disclaims any satirical or political meaning, but a family group of 1962 entitled *The Kennedys,* a figure resembling Lyndon Johnson, and another representing De Gaulle suggest that she does at times make comments on our society. Highly original both in her wit and in her use of mixed media, Marisol has become one of the most prominent younger American sculptors and has enjoyed great popularity with both the critics and the public. Major works of hers have been acquired by the Museum of Modern Art, the Whitney, and the Albright-Knox Art Gallery in Buffalo.

Niki de Saint Phalle was also born in Paris but grew up in New York, where she was a debutante. In the fifties she returned to Europe and began painting. Her most influential experience was seeing Gaudi's artificial trees and strange architectural forms in Barcelona in 1951 and the imaginary castle of a French mailman-artist in southern France. Inspired by these, she began working in plaster in which she embedded all kinds of found objects and strange shapes in order to create new and bizarre effects. Another of her ideas was to involve the public in her art, and she had people shoot guns at bags of pigment, thus creating instantaneous works of art. Her first show was at the Iolas Gallery in 1962, but she did not emerge as a mature artist until the later sixties when she produced her large Nana dolls. Using wire, strips of cloth, yarn, plaster, wool, and bright paint, she created images of great charm and humor. The figures of this type shown on the roof of the French Pavilion at Expo '67 in Montreal created a sensation and established Niki de Saint Phalle as one of the most gifted sculptors of her generation. Provoking laughter, protest, admiration, and strong audience participation, her work has been shown all over Europe and America. The most fantastic is her sixty-foot female figure called *L'Eloge de la Folie,* a walk-in sculpture she created for the Modern Museum in Stockholm. One hundred thousand people entered this "woman cathedral," which had a movie theatre in one arm and a milk bar in a breast. Other imaginative projects were a Nana-shaped sleeping dome built in southern France for her friend Rainer Diez and giant Nanas placed in the Bois de Boulogne in Paris.

Lee Bontecou is a native of Providence, Rhode Island, where she was born in 1931. She grew up in Nova Scotia and studied at the Art Students League with Zorach and Hovannes from 1952 to 1955. This was followed by a Fulbright in Rome and travels in Greece and Italy. Her first one-man show was in 1959, and she was included in the "Americans, 1963" show at the Museum of Modern Art where she achieved wide critical acclaim. Her mature works are completely unconventional in their use of materials and forms. Breaking away from the tradition of solid forms, she employs shaped canvas

[41]"Marisol," *Current Biography* (1968), p. 242.

<

Sky Cathedral 1972–1973, by Louise Nevelson, 20th century. *Pace Gallery, New York*

Women and Dog, by Marisol, 20th century. *Whitney Museum of American Art, New York*

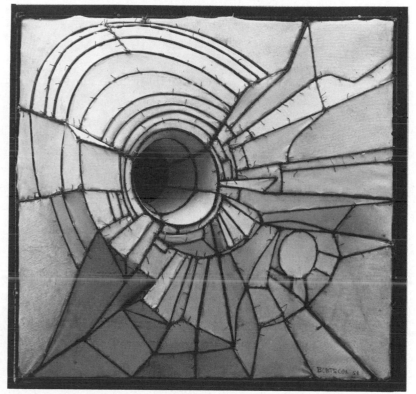

Black Venus, by Niki de Saint Phalle, 20th century. *Whitney Museum of American Art, New York*

Untitled sculpture of 1959 by Lee Bontecou, 20th century. *Smith College Museum of Art*

with wire frames that have sharp projecting forms and dark crevices. The result is strange and somehow menacing, creating a surreal, sometimes human, expression of a disturbing and haunting character. In talking about her work in 1960, Lee Bontecou said, "My concern is to build things that express our relationship to this country—to other countries—to this world—to other worlds—in terms of myself. To glimpse some of the fear, hope, ugliness, beauty and mystery that exists in us all and which hangs over all the young people today. The individual is welcome to see and feel in them what he wishes in terms of himself."[42]

[42]D. Miller, Catalogue of the Museum of Modern Art show, *Americans, 1963,* p. 12.

8 WOMEN GRAPHIC ARTISTS

FROM THE Renaissance on, a great many women artists have been active in graphic arts. In fact, in 1901 the Grolier Club of New York exhibited a large group of engravings, etchings, and lithographs that consisted entirely of works produced by women. Assembled in Holland, it is now part of the print collection of the New York Public Library. In fact, the print room of this library has no fewer than twenty-five hundred prints by women artists, making it probably the largest such collection in the world. Thousands of women have produced all kinds of graphic works over a period of some five hundred years, and yet, with the exception of Käthe Kollwitz and Mary Cassatt, it can hardly be said that their contribution is outstanding. Most of those who did produce fine prints were primarily painters who made prints as a sideline, usually not equaling the best of their work as painters, but this, of course, was also true of men.

The earliest recorded woman graphic artist is Ida van Meckenen, the wife of the late-fifteenth-century German printmaker Israel van Meckenen, who is said to have helped him in his workshop and managed his affairs. Professor Hildebrandt in his book on the woman as artist reproduces specific prints that he believes are by her and assigns to her the work of the so-called "Boccaccio engraver,"[43] but more cautious scholars do not think that it is possible to distinguish her work from that of her husband, although they agree that she was probably active in his workshop. As in

[43]H. Hildebrandt, *Die Frau als Künstlerin* (Berlin, 1928), p. 159 and plates 78 and 79.

painting, the early female printmakers were usually the wives or daughters of male artists who were able to offer them the training and facilities required for print making.

In Italy the best known of these early women graphic artists was Diana Sculptore, better known as Diana Ghisi. Born in Mantua in 1535, she was the daughter of the engraver and sculptor Giovanni Battista Sculptore. Vasari mentions Diana Ghisi, describing her as "a gentle and graceful child, who engraves remarkably well, her beautiful works amazing me." She was married to an architect, Francesco Capriani. About sixty of her engravings survive, most of them made after designs by other artists, notably Giulio Romano and the Roman Mannerists. While hardly original or important, her prints are skillfully executed and show the elegance and beauty characteristic of Italian Mannerist art. She died in Rome in 1588 at age fifty-three. During the seventeenth century, the outstanding Italian female printmaker was Elisabetta Sirani, who was also the daughter of an artist, namely, the Bolognese painter Giovanni Andrea Sirani. Born in Bologna in 1638, she studied with her father although she was primarily influenced by Guido Reni. She achieved early fame as an imitator of this master, receiving her first public commission at the age of seventeen. Although her life was cut short when she was poisoned by a servant in 1665, she produced a large number of paintings and etchings, largely of religious subjects done in a rather conventional Baroque style. While some of her prints are after Raphael, others are based on her own designs and combine an excellent use of chiaroscuro with a moving, somewhat sentimental depiction of sacred scenes and subjects such as the Holy Family.

During the eighteenth century a large number of women were active in the graphic arts. In France, producing prints became a favorite pastime of ladies of fashion, including even Madame de Pompadour, the mistress of Louis XV. Here again, some of the best graphic work was produced by artists who were primarily painters—Maria Sibylla Merian, for example, whose magnificent books of engravings of flowers, fruits, and insects are among the finest printed volumes of the late seventeenth and early eighteenth centuries, and Angelica Kauffmann, who made prints herself and had many prints made after her work. In England Maria Cosway, wife of the painter Richard Cosway, made some charming prints, but she too was primarily a painter and draftsman, and in Germany, Susanne Henry, the daughter of the German printmaker Daniel Chodowiecki, assisted her father and made some excellent prints of her own. The great bulk of female printmakers, however, were conventional, uninspired artists who worked in the fashionable styles of the day without distinguishing themselves either in excellence or uniqueness of vision.

It was not until the nineteenth century that two really outstanding female printmakers emerged: Kate Greenaway in England and Mary Cassatt in America. The former, born in Hoxton in 1846, was the daughter of the wood engraver John Greenaway who worked largely as a commercial illustrator for the *London Illustrated News* and *Punch* magazine. Her early years were spent in the country at Rolleston, and it has often been said that her art was inspired by her love of the countryside and the happy memories of her childhood. She showed early promise as an artist, winning a prize in the South Kensington Art School at the age of twelve. She studied drawing at various places, including the Slade School at University College in Oxford. Her watercolors were exhibited in London at the Dudley Gallery in 1868, when she was only twenty-two. In 1889 she was elected a member of the Institute of Painters of Watercolors, which at that time was a very prestigious institution. But she is best known for her illustrations. At first she did Christmas and Valentine cards—they had an

HAEC SENIOR, STERILIS PEPERIT VIRGO ALTERA, FOELIX
VTRAQVE, SED VATEM HAEC, EDIDIT ILLA DEVM

Holy Family, by Diana Sculptore, 16th century. *Fogg Museum, Harvard University*

Rest in Egypt, by Elisabetta Sirani, 17th century. *Fogg Museum, Harvard University*

Polly put the kettle on,
Polly put the kettle on,
Polly put the kettle on,
We'll all have tea.
Sukey take it off again,
Sukey take it off again,
Sukey take it off again,
They're all gone away.

K.G

Tom, Tom, the piper's son,
He learnt to play when he was young,
He with his pipe made such a noise,
That he pleased all the girls and boys.

K.G

"Polly put the kettle on," and "Tom, Tom, the piper's son," by Kate Greenaway in *The Annotated Mother Goose,* by W. S. Baring-Gould and C. Baring-Gould (New York: Clarkson N. Potter, Inc., 1962), pp. 152 and 257.

enormous commercial success—and then came the children's books, which have become classics in their field. She not only drew the pictures, she also wrote the rhymes and invented the process by which her drawings were reproduced photographically on wood. Her work consists largely of color wood engravings. Re-creating a world that was already old-fashioned when she made her illustrations, she imbued her characters with a charm that has appealed to many generations of children and that in her day created a tremendous vogue for her work. Her books made her rich and famous. To name but a few, there was *Under the Window,* her first great success, which was published in 1879, *Birthday Book, Mother Goose, A Child's Life,* and *The Language of Flowers.* Kate Greenaway was not just popular, she was also genuinely admired as an artist. Ruskin corresponded with her, the Crown Princess and later Empress of Germany sought her acquaintance, she was received at Buckingham Palace, and her fame spread to France and Germany. Her achievement is perhaps best summarized by the concluding paragraph of her entry in *The British Biographical Dictionary:*

> Technically Kate Greenaway was not a great artist, but she influenced greatly the art of the nineteenth century. In a limited sense she was the founder of a school, but she will be chiefly remembered for the revolution which she accomplished in the dress of the children of two continents. Her name has passed, not only into the English language but into the French, where "greenawisme" has gone to stay.

Her books were so successful financially that she was able to have the well-known architect Norman Shaw build her a house in Hampstead in 1885 and it was there that she lived until her death in 1901.

Very different in every respect was the American printmaker Mary Cassatt. Although she was undoubtedly the most outstanding nineteenth-century American woman painter and, in the opinion of French critics, the greatest artist America has produced, there are those who find her prints even more remarkable, and it must be said that, though she has several male rivals who surpass her in painting, only Whistler is her equal when it comes to graphic arts. She made a good number of prints during her long career, but her fame as a printmaker rests largely on a relatively small group of aquatints in color that she produced during the years 1890 and 1891. These works are not only the finest color prints made in nineteenth-century America, they are among the masterpieces of graphic art. Interestingly enough, they were inspired by the exhibition of Japanese colored wood blocks that she had seen with Degas at L'École Nationale des Beaux-Arts in Paris in the spring of 1890. She had previously been interested in Japanese prints, but after this show she bought examples of some outstanding Japanese printmakers—Kiyonaga, Shunjo, Haranobu, Utamaro, Hokusai, and Hiroshige—and had them installed in a special gallery in her château. Profoundly influenced by their flat decorative colors, strong line, and beautiful designs, Mary Cassatt made a group of prints showing women with children and women dressing and making up, works that for beauty of drawing, delicacy of color, and excellence of design are equal to the works of the Japanese masters and surpass the color prints of any of her contemporaries.

By far the greatest female printmaker is Käthe Kollwitz, one of the few women artists who enjoy an international fame equal to that of the most celebrated male graphic artists. She is also quite exceptional in being an artist whose fame rests entirely upon her prints. The only other fields in which she was active were drawing and sculpture. Indeed, some of her three-dimensional works, especially the memorial for her son killed on the battlefield of Flanders during the First World War, are among her

most memorable achievements. She is also one of the very few artists whose work has a strong social and even political message, a message that, because of its deep human compassion, never becomes mere political propaganda.

Born in 1867 in Königsberg, East Prussia, she came from a most interesting family. Her father, an ardent Social Democrat, had first studied law but then took up the trade of stonemason and, later, housebuilder. Her mother was the daughter of a Protestant minister who had been expelled from the official state church and had founded the First Free Congregation whose services and rites were based on those of the early Christian communities. These two men were strong personalities with deep convictions, and there is no question that the young Käthe Schmidt was profoundly influenced by her father and maternal grandfather. She had a happy youth as a member of a large family consisting not only of brothers and sisters but the children of relatives and close friends as well. Her family recognized her talent early and encouraged her to be an artist. As she says in her memoirs, "From my childhood on my father had expressly wished me to be trained for a career as an artist, and he was sure that there would be no great obstacles to my becoming one. And so after I reached my fourteenth year he sent me to the best teachers in Königsberg. The first was Maurer the engraver; later I studied with Emil Neide."[44] Since she was a woman, she was not able to attend the Academy of Art in Königsberg, but instead went to Berlin where she entered an art school for women. There she was very fortunate in having as her teacher the talented Swiss artist Karl Stauffer-Bern, who was a friend of the sculptor and etcher Max Klinger and who at once recognized the young woman's gifts. It was through him that she was introduced to Klinger's prints, which had a great influence on her own work. Her training was completed in Munich where she studied from 1888 to 1889, but this South German city did not suit her temperament and, in any case, she had decided that painting was not her field. In 1890 she returned to her native city and took up graphic art. In the following year she married Karl Kollwitz, a doctor who had set up his practice in the poorest workers' district in Berlin, and it was in Berlin that she lived for virtually the rest of her life. In fact, she and her husband remained in the same apartment until the bombing that occurred during the Second World War. Fittingly enough, the street where they lived in the north of Berlin, Weissenburgerstrasse, has since been renamed Käthe Kollwitz Strasse. Her first great success came a few years later with the exhibition of her prints based on Gerhart Hauptmann's play, *The Weavers,* which had deeply impressed the young artist. A jury committee, including two of Germany's most illustrious artists, Adolf von Menzel and Max Liebermann, voted to give her the gold medal for her work, but the award was vetoed by the Kaiser. The following year, at the Dresden exhibit, she won a gold medal, and her work was acquired for the print collections of the Berlin and the Dresden museums. Thus did Käthe Kollwitz, who was then just thirty years old, achieve national recognition and become the most famous woman artist in Germany.

For the next fifty years, Käthe Kollwitz devoted herself to her work, producing some of the greatest etchings, lithographs, and woodcuts in the history of graphic arts. A stay in Paris in 1904 enabled her to study sculpture and to meet Rodin. In 1907 she won the Villa Romana Prize, which permitted her to spend a year in Florence and to visit Rome.

[44]H. Kollwitz, ed., *Diaries and Letters of Käthe Kollwitz* (Chicago: Henry Regnery Co., 1955), p. 37.

<

The Letter, by Mary Cassatt, 19th century. *Metropolitan Museum of Art, New York*

Sharpening the Scythe, by Käthe Kollwitz, 20th century. *Fogg Museum, Harvard University*

The leading Berlin art dealer, Paul Cassirer, gave her a large retrospective to celebrate her fiftieth birthday in 1917, and in 1919, after the establishment of the German Republic, she became the first woman to be appointed to the Prussian Academy of Art. In 1927 she was an official guest of the Soviet government at the tenth-anniversary celebration of the Russian revolution, and a year later she took over the master class for graphics at the Art Academy in Berlin, a position of great importance and a rare honor for a woman. Her last years were clouded by the Nazi regime, to which as a lifelong socialist and pacifist she was bitterly opposed. She left the Prussian Academy of Art in 1933 and was dismissed from her teaching position. In 1936 she was prohibited from exhibiting, in 1940 her husband died, and in 1942 her beloved grandson Peter was killed in action just as her own son Peter had been killed in the First World War. She died in Moritzburg near Dresden only a few days before the war ended. Her son Hans, writing about her last days, said,

> My last visit was on Good Friday 1945. I read Mother the Easter Story from the gospel of St. Matthew—which she knew as well as the text of a favorite oratorio. Then I read her the Easter Walk from Faust, which she so loved. Shattered by age though she was, she seemed like a queen in exile, she had a compelling kindness and dignity. That is the last memory I have of her. My daughter was at her bedside when she died on April 22, 1945. Her last words were: My greetings to all.[45]

Käthe Kollwitz's life work certainly forms one of the most remarkable graphic oeuvres of all times. She started with etchings executed in a detailed realistic style, still part of a nineteenth-century tradition and already showing her deep social concern. Later she took up lithography, a medium in which she did some of her finest works, notably a series of magnificent self-portraits. During the twenties she made very powerful modern woodcuts. In these works, Käthe Kollwitz proved that print making could be an art form as significant as painting or sculpture, and that a female artist was capable of doing work of great strength, originality, and quality. At the same time, Käthe Kollwitz was a woman of infinite kindness, filled with compassion especially for the poor and miserable. She was also devoted to her family, proving that a woman can be both a fine artist and a loving wife and mother.

Käthe Kollwitz's work has often been characterized as socially conscious art, and it is true that she dwelled upon the dark aspects of life. As she herself said, "The joyous side simply did not appeal to me." A friend of hers reports that when he commented on the beauty of the freshly fallen snow on the trees in the Berlin Tiergarten, she replied, "I cannot enjoy the beauty of the snow as long as anyone must freeze in the cold." Yet she emphatically denied that she was a "socialist" artist, maintaining that she chose her subjects only because scenes from the lives of workers seemed interesting and beautiful. "For me," she said, "the Königsberg longshoremen had beauty; the Polish jimkes on their grain ships had beauty; the broad freedom of movement in the gestures of the common people had beauty. Middle-class people held no appeal for me at all. Bourgeois life as a whole seemed to me pedantic. The proletariat, on the other hand, had a grandeur of manner, a breadth to their lives."[46]

Like Daumier, to whom she can perhaps be best compared, her social comment is

[45]H. Bittner, *Käthe Kollwitz* (New York, Thomas Yoseloff, Inc., 1959), p. 15.

[46]Kollwitz, *Käthe Kollwitz,* p. 43.

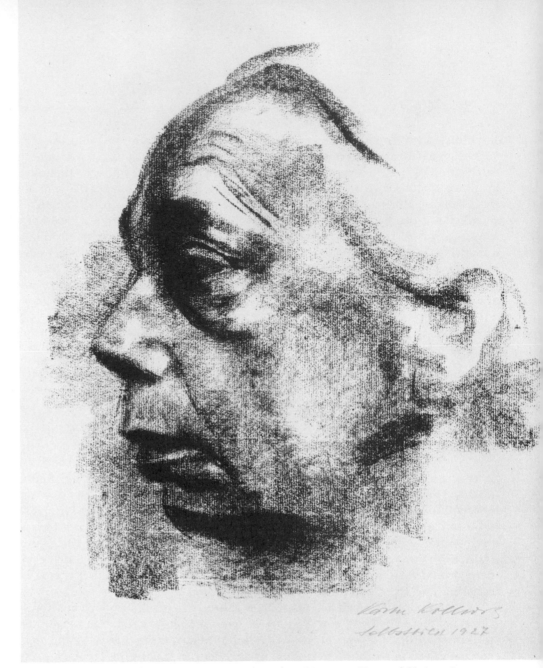

Self-portrait, by Käthe Kollwitz, 20th century. *Fogg Museum, Harvard University*

always the expression of deep human feeling. If she protests the horror of war, the degradation of the worker, the starvation of children, she does so not as a propagandist but as a human being with profound compassion for suffering humanity. Using bold, simple forms and reducing the image to its very essence, she expressed the tragedy and poverty of the people in universal and deeply moving terms. It is in this that her great strength lies. The only happy scenes she portrays are those dealing with the love between mothers and their children, and here her own maternal affection is clearly portrayed. Aside from these scenes, it is the darker side of life to which her art is almost exclusively dedicated. Among her most powerful works are the lithographs she made in her last years, in some of which she portrays the hand of death reaching for

E LEBENDEN DEM TOTEN . ERINNERUNG AN DEN 15. JANUAR 1919

Liebknecht Memorial, by Käthe Kollwitz, 20th century. *Fogg Museum, Harvard University*

her. Others are self-portraits in which, like Rembrandt, she shows the ravished features of the artist in old age. There are, of course, those who find Käthe Kollwitz's work too didactic, too gloomy, too conservative in technique, but her position as a graphic artist is more firmly established thirty years after her death than it was during her life. There is no doubt that she is one of the outstanding women artists of all times.

While Käthe Kollwitz devoted herself entirely to print making, the other significant female graphic artists of the twentieth century were mostly painters or sculptors who also did some prints. Virtually all the outstanding women painters made prints or book illustrations. Suzanne Valadon, whose drawings had been praised by Degas, did some fine aquatints, etchings, and drypoints, largely of nudes in a bold, linear style. Marie

Nudes under Trees, by Suzanne Valadon, 20th century. *Smith College Museum of Art*

>

Juliette, by Marie Laurencin, 20th century. *Smith College Museum of Art*

116

Laurencin did numerous etchings and lithographs in the delicate, graceful style associated with her painting, and she was particularly outstanding as an illustrator of novels. Among them were Gide's *La Tentative Amoureuse,* Dumas's *Camille,* and several English classics. Sonia Delaunay made an album of abstract color lithographs, did some silk-screen prints in a bold colorful style, and illustrated the poems of Tristan Tzara with color etchings.

In Germany, Paula Modersohn-Becker and Gabriele Münter both made prints. The former did ten etchings in an expressionistic style; the latter excelled in woodcuts in a simple, peasant manner. Yet, for both this was a minor aspect of their art. Far more important in their total work were the prints of two South Americans, Vieira da Silva and Leonor Fini, both of whom made numerous prints. Those of Vieira da Silva are etchings representing imaginary dream landscapes in complex intricate lines, whereas Leonor Fini is memorable for her elegant surrealist book illustrations.

Among American female artists of the twentieth century, the strongest graphic artist is not a painter but the sculptor Louise Nevelson, who has made some of the best prints to come out of America during this period. Working at Stanley William Hayter's Atelier 17, as several other leading women artists had done, she received instruction in etching in 1947, but she did not find the atmosphere very congenial. As she said later, "There were so many tools to use on this line and that field that I wondered if I was learning to make etchings or to become a surgeon."[47] But as a result of this experience she produced a group of etchings during the early fifties in which abstractly rendered human figures are drawn in white against a black background. Prints like *Night Figures, Flower Queen,* and *Pensive Figure* show her as a graphic artist of great strength and originality. Her second encounter with this medium came in 1963 when she was invited to go to the Tamarind Lithography Work Shop in Los Angeles on a Ford Foundation grant. The result was a series of powerful lithographs in black and white, with occasional use of deep blue and Indian red. Again the images are human figures in black fields. Rendered in a bleak, melancholy mood, they reflect her own state of mind at that period. They stand in striking contrast to her third series of prints, made during the seventies, in which colorful abstract shapes are used very effectively to create prints of rare beauty and sensibility.

[47]A. Glimcher, ed., *Louise Nevelson* (New York: Frederick A. Praeger, 1972), p. 63.

Double Imagery, by Louise Nevelson, 20th century. *Pace Gallery, New York*

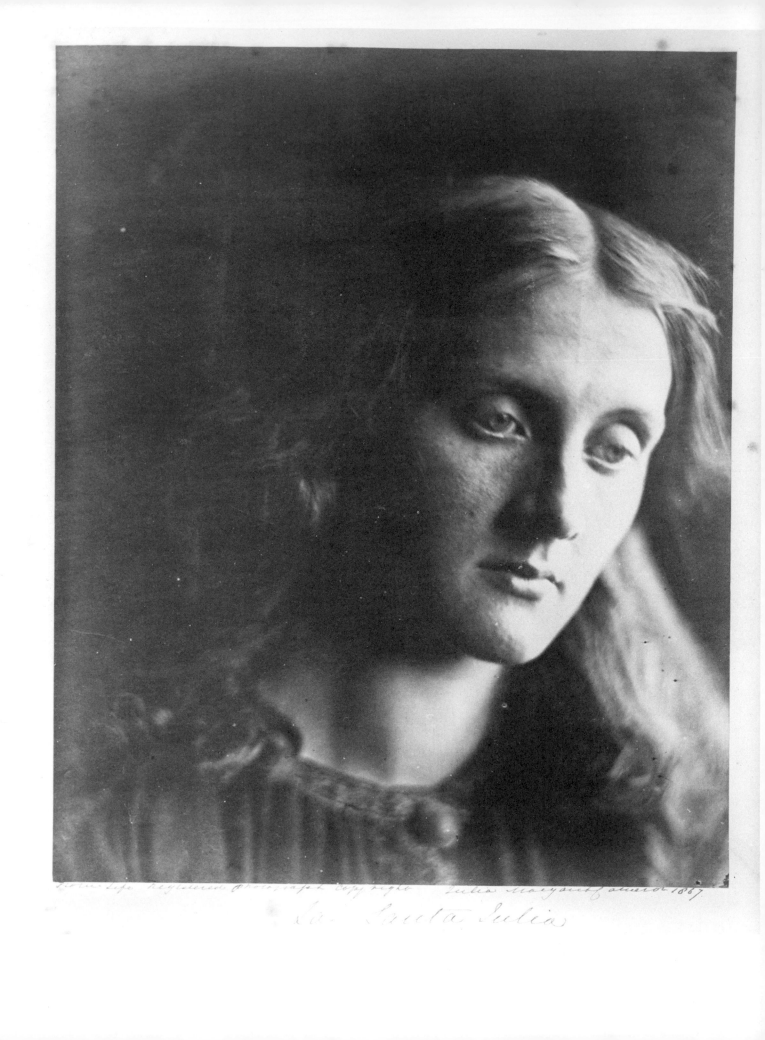

S.a Sancta Iulia — Julia Margaret Cameron, 1867

$\mathcal{9}$ WOMEN PHOTOGRAPHERS

THERE CAN be little doubt that women artists have been most prominent in photography and that they have made their greatest contribution in this field. One reason for this is not difficult to ascertain. As several historians of photography have pointed out, photography, being a new medium outside the traditional academic framework, was wide open to women and offered them opportunities that the older fields did not. As an ad in the *British Journal of Photography* said a hundred years ago in urging upon women the career of photographic assistant, "It is an occupation exactly suited to the sex, there are no great weights to carry, no arduous strain of body or mind, it is neat and clean."[48] Other articles stress that being a photographer takes little training and is a profession not restricted in the way many others are. John Szarkowski in his *Looking at Photographs* summarizes the case very well when he says,

> The importance of women as photographers has been much greater than one would guess on the basis of a straight statistical projection. As a nonscientific measure of this claim, it might be observed that the work of at least thirteen women is included among the one hundred pictures in this book, a percentage which is surely larger than that of women among those seriously committed to photography during most of the period involved. There are several possible explanations for the fact that women have been more important to photography than their numbers alone would warrant. One expla-

[48]H. Gernsheim, *History of Photography* (London: Oxford University Press, 1955), p. 401.

<

La Santa Julia (Mrs. Herbert Duckworth), by Julia Margaret Cameron, 1867. *Wellesley College Art Museum, Wellesley, Massachusetts*

nation might be the fact that photography has never had licensing laws or trade unions, by means of which women might have been effectively discriminated against. A second reason might be the fact that the specialized technical preparation for photography need not be enormously demanding, so that the medium has been open to those unable to spend long years in formal study.[49]

It might also be added that photography lends itself more readily to being practiced part time and at home. As a matter of fact there are many women photographers who have been able to combine being a wife and mother with being active and successful photographers, sometimes using their kitchen as a photographic darkroom.

All these observations apply to the first woman to have achieved eminence in photography, and that is Julia Margaret Cameron, whose portraits Beaumont Newhall in his *History of Photography* rightly calls "among the most noble and impressive yet produced by means of the camera."[50] Born in 1815 in Calcutta into an upper-middle-class family and married to Charles Hay Cameron, a distinguished jurist and member of the Supreme Court of India, Julia Cameron was well known as a brilliant conversationalist and a woman of personality and intellect who was unconventional to the point of eccentricity. Although the mother of six children, she adopted several more and still found time to be active in social causes and literary activities. After the Camerons settled in England in 1848 at Freshwater Bay on the Isle of Wight, she became the center of an artistic and literary circle that included such notable figures as the poet Alfred Lord Tennyson and the painter George Frederick Watts. Pursuing numerous activities and taking care of her large family, Mrs. Cameron might have been remembered as still another rather remarkable and colorful Victorian lady had it not been for the fact that, in 1863, her daughter presented her with photographic equipment, thinking her mother might enjoy taking pictures of her family and friends. Although forty-eight years old, Mrs. Cameron took up this new hobby with enormous enthusiasm and dedication. She was a complete beginner, but within a very few years she developed into one of the greatest photographers of her period and a giant in the history of photography. She worked ceaselessly as long as daylight lasted and mastered the technical processes of photography, at that time far more cumbersome than today, turning her coal house into a darkroom and her chicken house into a studio. To her, photography was "a divine art" and in it she found her vocation. In 1864 she wrote triumphantly under one of her photographs, "My First Success," and from then until her death in Ceylon in 1874 she devoted herself wholly to this art.

Working in a large format (her portrait studies are usually about 11 inches by 14 inches) and requiring a long exposure (on the average five minutes), she produced a large body of work that stands up as one of the notable artistic achievements of the Victorian period. The English art critic Roger Fry believed that her portraits were likely to outlive the works of artists who were her contemporaries; and her friend Watts, then a very celebrated portrait painter, inscribed on one of her photographs, "I wish I could paint such a picture as this." In a letter of 1866 he wrote, "Her work will satisfy posterity that there lived in 1866 an artist as great as Venice knew."[51] Her work was

[49]J. Szarkowski, *Looking at Photographs: 100 Pictures from the Collection of the Museum of Modern Art* (New York: The Museum of Modern Art, 1973), p. 52. Reprinted by permission.
[50]B. Newhall, *The History of Photography: From 1839 to the Present Day* (New York: The Museum of Modern Art, 1964), p. 64. Reprinted by permission.
[51]Gernsheim, *History of Photography,* p. 306.

widely exhibited, and she received gold, silver, and bronze medals in England, America, Germany, and Austria. No other female artist of the nineteenth century achieved such acclaim and no other woman photographer has ever enjoyed such success.

Her work falls into two main categories on which her contemporaries and people today differ sharply. Victorian critics were particularly impressed by her allegorical pictures, many of them based on the poems of her friend and neighbor Tennyson, and they often found her portraits "too truthful, even ugly."[52] Contemporary taste much prefers her portraits and finds her narrative scenes sentimental and sometimes in bad taste. Yet, not only Julia Cameron but the painters of that time loved to depict subjects such as *The Five Foolish Virgins* or *Pray God, Bring Father Safely Home.* Still, today her fame rests upon her portraits for, as she herself said, she was intent upon representing not only the outer likeness but also the inner greatness of the people she portrayed. Working with the utmost dedication, she produced photographs of such eminent Victorians as Tennyson, Browning, Carlyle, Trollope, Longfellow, Watts, Darwin, Ellen Terry, Sir John Herschel, who was a close friend of hers, and Mrs. Duckworth, the mother of Virginia Woolf. These photographs are among the greatest ever made and should answer the question once and for all whether photography is a fine art and whether women are capable of artistic achievements equal to those of men.

In the United States the first eminent woman photographer was Gertrude Käsebier. Born Gertrude Stanton in Des Moines, Iowa, in 1852, she grew up among simple frontier people and as a child crossed the plains in a covered wagon. After the death of her father, she moved east and lived first with her grandmother and then with her mother who ran a boardinghouse in New York City. In 1874 she married Eduard Käsebier, a native of Germany, with whom she had three children. Although interested in the arts from childhood, she did not seriously pursue a career until her children were grown up. At that point, she entered Pratt Institute in Brooklyn and studied portrait painting. However, she did not find her real vocation until she discovered the camera. This happened in 1893 during a trip to Europe, and is described vividly by the artist. One rainy day in a French provincial town, unable to go out and paint, she made several portraits with her camera.

> I had no conveniences for work, no darkroom, no running water in the house. Owing to the long twilight, I could not begin developing before ten o'clock. I had to carry my wet plates down to the river Brie to be washed. My way was through a winding path, with a tangle of overhanging branches, through a darkness so dense I could not see a step before me. It was often two o'clock in the morning, or almost dawn, when I had finished. I could not avoid dragged skirts and wet feet. More than one friend predicted I would get my death.[53]

Feeling a need for more technical training, she apprenticed herself to a German chemist who taught her photographic processes, and later she studied with a commercial portraitist in Brooklyn. In 1897 she set herself up as a portrait photographer in spite of her husband's reluctance to have her do so, and within a very short time became one of the most successful photographic artists in New York. Her work was reproduced in *Camera Notes* and *Camera Work,* the pioneering art-photography

[52]Ibid., p. 250.
[53]A. Tucker, *The Woman's Eye* (New York: Alfred A. Knopf, Inc., 1974), pp. 14–15.

Sir John Herschel, by Julia Margaret Cameron, 1867.
Metropolitan Museum of Art, New York

The Mountain Nymph, Sweet Liberty, by Julia Margaret
Cameron, 1866. *Metropolitan Museum of Art, New York*

magazines edited by Alfred Stieglitz; she exhibited at the Camera Club and Stieglitz's
famous "291" Gallery; was one of the founders of the Photo Secessionist movement. She
won numerous medals, awards, and citations at American and international exhibitions,
and died in 1934 at age eighty-two.

Gertrude Käsebier worked in the pictorial style that was very much in vogue during
the last years of the nineteenth and the first decade of the twentieth centuries. Like the
other photographers of this movement, she tried to get effects closely related to those of
Impressionist painting. Although she did many portraits, her most important work
consists of poetic, pictorial compositions, many of them related to motherhood, a theme
in which she was particularly interested. Other outstanding works are her photographs
of American Indians and Buffalo Bill's Wild West Show, as well as her pictures of
Auguste Rodin and his work, which she made in 1907. At their best, her soft-focus
photographs, especially those of women and children, have a lyrical charm and
suggestiveness, and these qualities established her as the most famous American

Blessed Art Thou among Women, by Gertrude Käsebier, circa 1900. *Collection of Library of Congress, Washington, D.C.*

Mother and Child, by Gertrude Käsebier, 20th century. *Collection of Library of Congress, Washington, D.C.*

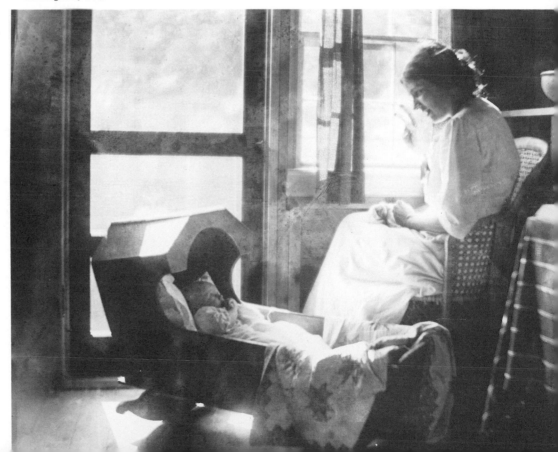

woman artist of her day. However, as this style of photography went out of fashion her fame declined, and during the later years of her life, when a documentary style of photography became popular, her work seemed old-fashioned and insipid. Yet, the best pictures of her huge output, which is estimated at one hundred thousand prints, are among the highest achievements of pictorial photography.

Very different both in temperament and photographic style is the other leading woman photographer of the late nineteenth and early twentieth centuries, Frances Benjamin Johnston. Born in 1864 in Grafton, West Virginia, and reared in Rochester, New York, and Washington, D.C., she studied painting and drawing at the Académie Julian in Paris and at the Art Students League in Washington. Her first job was as a correspondent for a New York magazine, and it was through this reportorial work that she was led to photography, initially simply to illustrate her articles. Her first photographs were of such subjects as the United States Mint, the Pennsylvania coal fields, and homes of the President, the members of Congress, and the diplomatic corps, which were published in *Demorest's Family Magazine* in 1889 and 1890. In the early nineties she set herself up as a portrait photographer in Washington, D.C., and became well known as an eccentric but able professional. A friend of Gertrude Käsebier and a member of the New York Camera Club, she exhibited in the pictorial photography salons. However, real success only came in 1899 when she was commissioned to photograph the school system of Washington, D.C., and the Hampton Institute in Virginia with its community. These works, first shown at the Paris Exposition of 1900, won a gold medal and established her as the finest documentary photographer of her time. Unlike Gertrude Käsebier, who was primarily interested in pictorial effects, Frances Johnston, who was an early fighter for women's rights and worked to "improve the Negro's lot," saw her art as a tool in this struggle. As one of the few women delegates to the International Photographic Congress in Paris, she delivered a lecture on women photographers of America and wrote a series of articles on the same subject for the *Ladies' Home Journal.* She continued throughout her life an active and successful professional career, which culminated in a beautiful series of 7,648 pictures depicting the early architecture of the southern states. She took the pictures between 1933 and 1940 when she was a woman in her seventies. She died in 1952 at age eighty-eight.

Frances Johnston's great contribution to the art of photography, although appreciated during her life, was forgotten until the Museum of Modern Art published and exhibited photographs from her Hampton album in 1966. After this exhibition had been shown widely throughout the country, her place as one of the outstanding documentary photographers was assured. Recording the scene in front of her with great precision and honesty, she produced an invaluable record of America, its institutions and people, a record that is not only historically important but also artistically of the highest order. The quality that distinguishes her from latter-day photojournalists is her fine sense of classical composition. Because she had been trained as a painter in the academic manner, Frances Johnston, although intent upon recording the reality in front of her, was always very concerned with formal arrangements, whether in depicting people or buildings. This is particularly true of her Hampton photographs, in which she often poses her subjects in carefully constructed groups, creating a beautiful formal design that a mere record of the scene would not have produced.

The third and youngest of these great women photographers was Imogen Cunningham. A native of Portland, Oregon, where she was born in 1883, she has spent her entire life on the West Coast. When she was six her family moved to Seattle, and it

A HISTORY OF WOMEN ARTISTS

Testing at Hampton Institute, Virginia, by Frances Benjamin Johnston, 1899. *Collection of Library of Congress, Washington, D.C.*

Hayes House, Edenton, North Carolina, by Frances Benjamin Johnston, 1937. *Collection of Library of Congress, Washington, D.C.*

Plant forms, by Imogen Cunningham, 1923. *Courtesy Witkin Gallery, New York*

was there that she grew up and attended the University of Washington. The decisive moment in her life came in 1901 when she saw a reproduction of Gertrude Käsebier's work and decided to become a photographer. Her father, who had wanted her to be a schoolteacher, did not approve of this career and could not see any reason for her to continue her education if she was going to be "just a dirty photographer." However, she persevered and after graduating from the university, where she majored in chemistry, she worked in the Curtis Studio in order to learn commercial platinum printing. In 1909 she went to Germany where she studied at the Technical College in Dresden, which was well known for its department of photographic chemistry.

Upon her return to Seattle she opened a portrait studio as Gertrude Käsebier and Frances Johnston had done. Her early work reflects on the one hand the romantic, soft-focus style fashionable at the time, and on the other hand, especially in her portraits, a new more direct approach to her subjects. In 1915 she married a fellow artist, the etcher Roi Partridge, and had three sons. The couple lived first in Seattle and then in San Francisco and Oakland. Although she was a devoted wife and mother, she continued her photographic work, more for her own satisfaction than as a profession. As her children grew up, she returned to photography full time and in 1930 became one of the founding members of the F/64 group, which included her friends Edward Weston and Ansel Adams. Her work has been widely exhibited and reproduced in many prestigious magazines, and in 1967 she was one of only two women, the other being Martha Graham, who was made a fellow of the National Academy of Arts and Sciences. Retrospectives of her work have been held in numerous museums, most notably at the George Eastman House in Rochester in 1961, the San Francisco Museum of Art in 1961, the Chicago Art Institute in 1964, the Henry Gallery of the University of Washington in 1965, and the Stanford University Art Gallery in 1967. In 1968 she received an honorary doctor's degree from the California College of Arts and Crafts.

Imogen Cunningham's photographs are mostly of people or close-ups of natural forms like flowers, plants, and leaves. She rarely photographs larger scenes, but focuses with great precision on specific forms. While she, too, started as a pictorial photographer who was trying to achieve painterly effects, her mature work, beginning in 1920, uses a sharp-focus camera and represents visual reality in a very direct and simple manner. Her series on plants, made during the twenties, with their beautiful clear forms and fine sense of design are works of especially great beauty and originality. Other works of unusual merit are her photographs of nudes seen in a highly abstract manner and the close-up of hands which brings to this subject a great sensitivity and clarity of vision. Yet, she is probably best known for her portrait studies, which she has continued to produce throughout her life. She took pictures of many of her famous contemporaries, such as Martha Graham, Gertrude Stein, Herbert Hoover, Upton Sinclair, Morris Graves, and, above all, her colleagues Edward Weston, Alfred Stieglitz, and Minor White, producing photographs combining beauty of design and execution with profound psychological interpretation. Today, at ninety, she is still active as a photographer, having outlived many of her juniors such as Dorothea Lange and Margaret Bourke-White. Her son Ron affectionately calls her "my hippie mother," and when she was asked to comment on her photographs, she said that there was far too much philosophizing about photography these days, adding, "People will just have to look at my stuff and make up their own minds."[54]

[54]M. Mann, *Imogen Cunningham* (Seattle, Washington, 1970), p. 6.

Schmitt mit dem Kuchenmesser, by Hannah Höch, 20th century. *National Gallery, Berlin*

Among German women artists working in photography, the Dadaist Hannah Höch was the most interesting. Born in 1889 into a middle-class family in Gotha, Germany, she went to Berlin in 1914 where she studied with Orlik, working in an Impressionist style. With brief interruptions during the First World War, and some years in Holland, she remained in Berlin all her life. By 1915 she had started painting in an abstract style based on Kandinsky and had become part of the avant-garde art movement in the German capital. Looking back on these years, she said,

> Thirty years ago it was not very easy for a woman to impose herself as a modern artist in Germany. . . . Most of our male colleagues continued for a long while to look upon us as charming and gifted amateurs, denying us implicitly any real professional status. Hans Arp and Kurt Schwitters, in my experience, were rare examples of the kind of artist who can really treat a woman as a colleague. But Arp is also one of the most inspired artists I have ever met.[55]

Although Hannah Höch was active until her death in 1971, her most creative years spanned the period from about 1916 until 1930, during which she was one of the central members of the Berlin Dada movement, along with George Grosz and Raoul Hausmann, with whom she was living at the time. Her particular contribution lay in the fields of photomontage and collage, in which she produced some of the most original and provocative works of the period. Juxtaposing different images and cutting up photographs and pasting them together in combinations, Hannah Höch created novel, often startling images which gave powerful expression to the chaos and discontent of those years. Although she was not the first to employ these devices, she was the one who used photomontage most effectively and for the longest period of time, starting as a Dadaist in 1916 when she was in her twenties, and continuing throughout her life.

While Hannah Höch was manipulating photographs and using images in new and startling ways, some of the leading American women photographers of the twentieth century were realists who wanted to show the world without fear or favor, letting their lens reflect what their eye saw. Among these documentary photographers none is finer than Dorothea Lange, whose work of the 1930s is the most honest, straightforward, and moving portrait of America of that time. Born in Hoboken, New Jersey, in 1895, Dorothea Lange grew up in a middle-class German-American family in New York City where she attended high school and a teacher-training school. But when she was twenty she decided to become a photographer and, on the advice of Arnold Genthe, with whom she had studied, she enrolled in 1917 in a photography course taught by Clarence White at Columbia University. A trip around the world was cut short in San Francisco when a thief stole all her money, and she settled down there and in 1919 opened a portrait studio. In the following year she married the painter Maynard Dixon with whom she had two sons.

It was not until the 1930s that Dorothea Lange emerged as a major photographer. Beginning with her 1933 photograph, *White Angel Breadline, San Francisco,* and the many photographs made for the California State Emergency Relief Administration and the Farm Security Administration, she emerged as a powerful and influential photographer. In 1939 she published jointly with Paul Taylor, her second husband, a book entitled *An American Exodus: A Record of Human Erosion.* It summarizes her particular contribution to photography by effectively combining her documentary photographs with a text made up in part of the sayings of the people she was portraying. Although she remained active for two more decades, photographing the Japanese evacuated from the West Coast, workers in the war industries, the Irish

[55]From an interview with Edouard Roditi, *Arts Magazine* (December 1959), p. 29.

Ex-slave and wife, Greene County, Georgia, by Dorothea Lange, 1937. *Collection of Library of Congress, Washington, D.C.*

country people, and the peoples of Asia, it is on these photographs of rural America during the depression that her fame chiefly lies. A large retrospective at the Museum of Modern Art in New York organized to honor her life work in 1966 became a memorial show when she died of cancer in 1965 at age seventy.

The words that best describe her work are the ones by Francis Bacon, which she herself chose and tacked on her darkroom door in 1923: "The contemplation of things as they are/Without error or confusion/Without substitution or imposture/Is in itself a nobler thing/Than a whole harvest of invention."[56]

It is this honesty and directness of vision that was her guiding principle. For her, photography was not a medium to achieve pictorial effects or pleasing formal designs, but a way of recording social reality with an emphasis on the poor and disenfranchised people of rural America. Portraying them with sympathy and understanding, she created deeply human and moving images that are among the most memorable to have come out of the depression years in America. Although her photographs of the migrant workers were instrumental in bringing their plight to the attention of the nation and the government, her pictures are never mere political propaganda. They are powerful precisely because of their uncompromising realism, which seems to say—Here are these people as they really are, victims of forces they do not control, feeling and experiencing life like you and me, and enduring in spite of all adversity.

The other outstanding American woman photographer of this period is Berenice Abbott. Three years younger than Dorothea Lange, she was born in 1898 in Springfield, Ohio. She went to school in Cleveland and for a year and a half attended Ohio State University. But in 1918 she decided to become an artist and she moved to New York where she studied sculpture. After three years, she went to Paris, where she studied under Bourdelle, and then in 1923 to Berlin, to attend the Art Academy. It was not until she worked in Man Ray's Paris studio that she decided to become a portrait photographer. The work of her Paris period, when she took pictures of famous literary and artistic figures of France such as André Gide, Jean Cocteau, James Joyce, Marcel Duchamp, Max Ernst, and Marie Laurencin, is among her finest, and established her reputation as one of the most gifted women artists of her generation.

Despite her great success in Paris, she left Europe in 1929 and returned to New York, where she became fascinated with the city and decided to photograph the life of this great metropolis "before the old buildings and historic spots were destroyed," just as her friend Atget, the great French photographer, had recorded Paris. The result was her greatest achievement, a huge number of pictures on every aspect of the city from the grandeur of the towering skyscrapers to the crowded tenements of the slums. A selection of the work, published in 1939 under the title *Changing New York,* at once established her reputation. Funded partly by the Federal Art Project and the Museum of the City of New York, where the negatives are now deposited, she recorded the city in photographs that are now classics. She is most famous for her pictures of New York City, although she later made many other excellent photographs, most notably the ones dealing with science and the scenic beauty of the Atlantic Coast region, particularly Maine, where she has made her home since 1968.

In addition to her creative work, Miss Abbott has also had an important influence on American photography through her teaching, especially at the New School of Social

[56]Quoted in Museum of Modern Art Catalogue of Exhibition of Dorothea Lange, New York, 1966, p. 6.

Research in New York, and her writing, for she wrote several manuals on photography; she also brought Atget's work to the attention of the American public. Her enormous collection of his negatives and photographs, which she purchased from his estate after his death and which is now in the collection of the Museum of Modern Art in New York, was the source of the portfolio she issued and served as the illustrations for her book *The World of Atget.* She has also served on many committees and juries, has taken a great interest in the work of younger photographers, and has encouraged women to enter this field of art.

Speaking of her own work and her ideas about what photography should be, she said,

Broome Street, New York, by Berenice Abbott, 1935. *Museum of the City of New York, New York*

A photograph is or should be a significant document, a penetrating statement, which can be described in a very simple term—selectivity. To define selection, one may say that it should be focused on the kind of subject matter which hits you hard with its impact and excites your imagination to the extent that you are forced to take it. . . . Selection of proper picture content comes from a fine union of trained eye and imaginative mind.[57]

It is precisely this quality of her work—realism combined with selectivity—that distinguishes it from the hundreds of thousands of photographs of New York taken by other, less talented, photographers. And while Dorothea Lange recorded the people of rural America and their environment, Berenice Abbott has caught for all time the rhythm of the American city with its splendor and its squalor, its bustling life and its areas of desolation and decay.

A contemporary of Lange and Abbott, although coming from a different background and leading a very different life, was Tina Modotti. Born in Undine, Italy, in 1886, the daughter of a carpenter, she spent her early life in Italy and Austria. Her father emigrated to the United States where she joined him in San Francisco in 1915. After working in a factory for a time, she became interested in the theatre and eventually got into the movies in Hollywood. The climax of her film career came in 1921 when she played in a movie called *Tiger Lady,* but in the same year she left for Mexico with her friend, the painter and poet Roubaix de l'Abri Richey. After her lover's death the following year, she returned to the United States where she met Edward Weston. It was Weston who introduced her to photography, which became her true form of expression. With him she returned to Mexico and during a brief period of five years, she made some of the finest pictures ever produced. Her work of these years was first shown, together with that of Weston, in 1924 in the Art Museum of Guadalajara, and was published in *Mexican Folkways.*

A passionate antifascist and for some years a member and perhaps even an agent of the Communist party, Tina Modotti broke with Weston and stayed in Mexico, devoting herself to revolutionary activities. In 1930 the Mexican government deported her because of her Communist activities and because she was believed to have been involved in the death of a friend of hers who was murdered by political opponents. Her later life is shrouded in mystery, with reports of her having been in the Soviet Union, where some of her work was reproduced in *International Literature,* in Spain during the Civil War, in Germany where she is said to have worked for the Communist party, and eventually back in Mexico where she died under mysterious circumstances in 1942. In the same year a retrospective of her work was held in the Museum of Modern Art in Mexico City.

Unlike the work of Lange and Abbott, which has been widely published and has been in the collections of leading museums for many years, that of Tina Modotti is still largely unknown and has seldom been exhibited or reproduced. Even after the publication of Edward Weston's *Day Books,* through which her face and something about her life became well known, much about her remains mysterious and no comprehensive exhibition of her work has been held. Although she was a political activist and was certainly intent upon recording the revolutionary forces in Mexico, what makes her photographs so moving is their deep humanity combined with a

[57]*Art of Photography* (New York: Time-Life Books, 1971), p. 20.

wonderful sense of artistic design equaling the work of Edward Weston at his best. In discussing her artistic philosophy, she said:

> Photography, precisely because it can only be produced in the present and because it is based on what exists objectively before the camera, takes its place as the most satisfactory medium of registering objective life in all its aspects, and from this comes its documental value. If to this is added sensibility and understanding above all, a clear orientation as to the place it should have in the field of historical development, I believe that the result is something worthy of a place in social production, to which we all contribute.[58]

She took close-ups of flowers and abstract architectural studies, but it is in her pictures of the common people of Mexico that Tina Modotti's finest work is to be found. Like the Russian director Eisenstein and his camera man Tisse in their film about Mexico, Modotti was able to catch something of the simple grandeur and dignity of the Mexican peasants. That sense of objective life she talked about is combined with a sensitive aesthetic feeling, creating images that are of the highest artistic order.

The most outstanding woman photojournalist and one of the most famous photographers who has ever lived was Margaret Bourke-White. She was born in New York in 1904, the daughter of the naturalist, engineer, and inventor Joe White and his wife Minnie Bourke. Her college years were spent chiefly at Cornell, from which she graduated in 1927, but she also studied photography under Clarence White at Columbia. Her earliest photographs, taken on the Ithaca campus, sold well, and after her father died and her early marriage ended in divorce, she decided to become a professional photographer. She first distinguished herself by doing free lance industrial photography in Cleveland. This brought her to the attention of Henry Luce, who hired her for the magazine *Fortune* in 1929. She worked six months a year for Luce doing many notable photo essays on American industry, and for the rest of the year she worked free lance on advertising assignments. But her great opportunity came in 1936 when she joined the new magazine *Life,* for she is best remembered as one of the most enterprising and accomplished of *Life*'s photojournalists, who, as has been said, always managed to be at the right place at the right time. She photographed Russia during the Battle of Moscow and Gandhi shortly before his assassination, and was with Patton when he liberated the concentration camp at Buchenwald. She was torpedoed off North Africa, was in a helicopter crash in Korea, and went through the bombings of the Second World War. Her energy and courage were legendary; no assignment was too difficult and she worked at each of her tasks with the same unfailing enthusiasm and dedication. Her pictures in *Life* made her internationally famous and gave her the greatest exposure any woman photographer has ever had. Many of the pictures were also published in book form, for, despite her busy schedule, she wrote six books about her experiences: an autobiography, and four books in collaboration with other authors, notably *You Have Seen Their Faces,* which she coauthored in 1937 with Erskine Caldwell, to whom she was married from 1939 to 1942. After this active and productive life, her last years were filled with suffering, which she bore with characteristic fortitude and recorded both in word and in film. In 1952 she noticed a dull ache in her left leg; it proved to be the first symptom of

[58]Lee Edwards, ed., *Women, An Issue* (Boston: Houghton Mifflin Co., 1972), p. 115.

<

Mexican woman, "Elisa," by Tina Modotti, 1924. *The Museum of Modern Art, New York (gift of Edward Weston)*

Parkinson's disease, but this was undiagnosed for several years. The disease got worse, and therapeutic exercises proved useless. In 1958 the condition was recognized and two operations were undertaken, but, in spite of her heroic struggle, the disease recurred. She spent the last three years of her life in a hospital and died in 1971 at age sixty-seven.

Margaret Bourke-White was the very essence of a photographer who is a journalist working with pictures instead of words. Using dramatic shots to convey the sense of excitement and drama that she herself felt, and always being at the place where the action was, she was a true professional, and the equal of any man. Yet, looking at her pictures decades later, when the thrill and interest of a particular event have more or less subsided, we find her work to be somewhat dated and topical. It is her moving photographs of the sharecroppers of the rural South in *You Have Seen Their Faces* that stand up best and in which she most fully achieves the kind of truth she said she was searching for. As she said, "To get that truth may take a lot of seeking and long hours." And yet Margaret Bourke-White, always a professional and a perfectionist, was willing to spend those long hours, and in these pictures produced some masterpieces of photography.

Helen Levitt, whose lyrical evocations of New York in the 1940s are works of rare beauty, is the very opposite of Margaret Bourke-White. A native of New York City, she began her career as a photographer of Harlem in 1936. Trained by Walker Evans and inspired by the work of Henri Cartier-Bresson, Helen Levitt has developed her own style of descriptive photography, which gives a vivid account of life on the streets of New York without becoming journalistic. In 1941 she went to Mexico where she photographed the country and the people.

Her great gifts were recognized early by the Museum of Modern Art in New York, which in 1943 gave her a one-man show entitled "Children." In 1946 she received a grant to take pictures of New York, and the result was a book of photographs with a text by James Agee called *A Way of Seeing*, an imaginative and poetical portrait of New York. In it, portraying the games of children and the activities of adults, she brings to these scenes a fresh and responsive eye. As John Szarkowski says so eloquently,

> What is remarkable about the photographs is that these immemorially routine acts of life, practiced everywhere and always, are revealed as being full of grace, drama, humor, pathos and surprise, and also that they are filled with the qualities of art, as though the street were a stage, and its people were all actors and actresses, mimes, orators and dancers.[59]

Diane Arbus, now the most famous woman photographer who worked in the 1960s, was a highly original artist whose photographic images have a compelling fascination. She was born in 1923 into a well-to-do Jewish family in New York. Her father, David Nemerov, was the owner of the woman's fashion store called Russek's, and her brother Howard was a poet. She went to the Ethical Culture and Fieldston schools. At eighteen she married Allan Arbus, whom she had met when she was fourteen. The couple had two girls. Both Diane Arbus and her husband became fashion photographers and worked for her father. After some twenty years she decided to quit and devote herself to creative photography. In 1959 she began to study with Lisette Model and, during the last

[59]Szarkowski, *Looking at Photographs*, p. 138.

<

Two women in Lansdale, Arkansas, from *You Have Seen Their Faces* by Margaret Bourke-White, 1937. *Permission of Time-Life*

ten years of her life, she devoted herself entirely to her own photography. In 1963 she received a Guggenheim Fellowship for a project she called "The American Experience," and a second one was given to her in 1966. However, she was very reluctant to show her work and was hardly known in 1971 when she killed herself by slashing her wrists. She was forty-eight years old.

A year later, when the Museum of Modern Art gave her a major exhibition and Aperture, Inc., published a monograph on her work, Diane Arbus became the object of a cult. Her brother Howard wrote a poem to her called "To D . . . Dead by Her Own Hand" which appeared in *Poetry* magazine and the *Saturday Review of Literature.* She was the first photographer to be shown at the Venice Biennale, where ten of her pictures, enormously blown up, were the sensation of the American Pavilion, and her retrospective at the Museum of Modern Art was seen by seventy thousand people in the first twenty days (seven thousand on a single Sunday), making it one of the most successful exhibitions ever shown at the museum.

Maureen, by Judy Dater, 1971. *Courtesy Witkin Gallery, New York*

Hilton Kramer, writing about this phenomenon, called her one of those rare artists "who suddenly, by a daring leap into a territory formerly regarded as forbidden, altered the terms of the art she practiced." What made her unique was her subject matter, usually freaks and misfits, rather than any artistic or technical contribution. As she herself said,

> Freaks was a thing I photographed a lot. It was one of the first things I photographed and it has had a terrific kind of excitement for me. I just used to adore them. I still do adore some of them—I don't quite mean they are my best friends but they make me feel a mixture of shame and awe. There's a quality of legend about freaks. Like a person in a fairy tale who stops you and demands that you answer a riddle. Most people go through life dreading they'll have a traumatic experience. Freaks were born with their trauma. They've already passed their test in life. They're aristocrats.[60]

There is no doubt that the artist was drawn to what was weird and at times repulsive, and even when she photographed ordinary people, she made them seem strange and disturbing, perhaps projecting onto them something of her own feeling about life. As she said, she felt a deep sympathy and even identification with her subjects, whom she befriended and liked. No doubt her response to them inspired their confidence. To the onlooker they seem pitiful misfits, the outcasts of society, but for Diane Arbus they were people of interest and dignity. Photographed in a very straightforward style that deliberately avoided artful effects, she recorded them as they appeared and it may be that the fascination of her work lies in this uncompromising honesty.

The most gifted of America's young women photographers now working is Judy Dater. Her work is only beginning to receive the recognition it deserves, but the exhibition of her work at the Witkin Gallery in New York in 1974 aroused considerable interest. A native of southern California, where she was born in 1941, she attended the University of California in Los Angeles and in 1962 transferred to San Francisco State College to study photography. Working with a variety of subjects, she did landscapes, still lifes, buildings, and street scenes; later, she concentrated on people, especially women. She became a founding member of a California-based group of photographers called the Visual Dialogue Foundation. Most of them are graduates of San Francisco State College. In 1971 she married the photographer Jack Welpott with whom she had worked since the middle sixties. With him she did a series of pictures on urban women, and this constitutes her most significant work to date.

Unlike Diane Arbus, who made a cult of not being artistic or posing her figures, Judy Dater carefully poses her subjects, hoping that by their dress and their environment she will bring out their personality. Her world is the world of the bohemian intelligentsia of contemporary California. They are the present-day liberated women of America, self-consciously displaying their sexuality and presenting themselves to the onlooker in a sophisticated way. And yet for all their feminine allure, there is something disturbing and rather morbid about them as if they, too, to paraphrase A. E. Housman, were strangers and afraid in a world they never made. However, it is precisely this quality in Judy Dater's work, as well as its artistic excellence, that most appeals.

[60]Diane Arbus, *Diane Arbus* (New York: Aperture, 1972), p. 3.

10 CONCLUSIONS AND OBSERVATIONS

HAVING SURVEYED the history of women's art, we must ask ourselves if it is possible to come to any conclusion about women's contribution to art or to formulate any generalizations about women in the visual arts. The radical feminist point of view is forcefully expressed by Linda Nochlin in her essay "Why Have There Been No Great Women Artists?" She says, "The fact of the matter is that there have been no supremely great women artists, as far as we know, although there have been many interesting and very good ones who remain insufficiently investigated or appreciated." She gives the following explanation for this:

> But in actuality, as we all know, things as they are and as they have been, in the arts as in a hundred other areas, are stultifying, oppressive, and discouraging to all those, women among them, who did not have the good fortune to be born white, preferably middle-class and, above all, male. The fault, dear brothers, lies not in our stars, our hormones, our menstrual cycles or our empty internal spaces, but in our institutions and our education—education understood to include everything that happens to us from the moment we enter this world of meaningful symbols, signs, and signals. The miracle is, in fact, that given the overwhelming odds against women, or blacks, that so many of both have managed to achieve so much sheer excellence, in those bailiwicks of white masculine prerogative like science, politics or the arts.[61]

[61]Linda Nochlin, "Why Have There Been No Great Women Artists?" *Art News* (January, 1971), p. 25.

This point of view is at best a contention that can hardly stand up to serious scrutiny when examined in any but the most general way. Though it is true that there have been no female Michelangelos, Rembrandts, or Cézannes, Linda Nochlin's contention that there have been "no women equivalents . . . in very recent times, for de Kooning or Warhol" is one with which most critics and women artists would certainly disagree. It must also be said that geniuses like Michelangelo are extremely rare, and that their extraordinary gifts are hardly the result of greater professional opportunities or better training. After all, thousands of their fellow artists have ended up obscure or forgotten, just as most women artists have. The equivalent would be to maintain that since there were no British rulers equal to Queen Elizabeth or no French saints equal to Joan of Arc, this proved that men did not have the same opportunities that women enjoyed. At the same time, no one would dispute that there have been many outstanding women artists and that Georgia O'Keeffe as a painter, Julia Cameron as a photographer, Käthe Kollwitz as a printmaker, and Louise Nevelson as a sculptor are not derivative and not second-rate but are comparable to the most gifted of their male contemporaries. And what is one to make of the fact that, under similar social and cultural conditions, women have achieved positions of far greater eminence in literature than in the visual arts but have not distinguished themselves in music? Certainly Sappho in antiquity and, above all, Lady Murasaki in medieval Japan were able to equal and even surpass the male writers of their periods, with the *Tale of Genji* to this day considered the greatest novel in Japanese literature and one of the supreme literary masterpieces of all times. And would any one care to maintain that Jane Austen, the Brontës, and Virginia Woolf are second-rate when compared to their male contemporaries? Or that Emily Dickinson is not as original as any nineteenth-century American poet? Certainly no one could claim that there were any circumstances in their lives that gave Jane Austen, the Brontës, or Emily Dickinson advantages that contemporary women do not enjoy. In fact, the contrary was the case, and yet their creativity found an outlet even against overwhelming odds. Is it not more likely that, for some reason, women are more gifted verbally than visually? And that in music, although they have excelled in playing instruments and singing, they have never shown any particular talent as composers? If artistic excellence was determined by institutions and education, would not the twentieth century have produced increasing numbers of outstanding female artists as women achieved ever greater equality in all areas of life? The fact is that this has not been true except in sculpture, where women had few opportunities prior to the modern age. Certainly no twentieth-century painter has had the fame and success Elisabeth Vigée-Lebrun and Angelica Kauffmann enjoyed two centuries ago nor is any contemporary woman artist as celebrated as Rosa Bonheur at the height of her career. Yet, the number of women active in the arts is greater than ever. The art schools and the art departments are crowded with aspiring female artists, but is this any guarantee for excellence? And were there not, as Linda Nochlin herself contended, thousands of women painters in Victorian England alone?

A very different view of female artists, which was particularly popular in the late Victorian period, was that women artists had a peculiarly feminine quality that distinguished their work from that of men. This sentiment is expressed in Walter Sparrow's discussion of the work of Vigée-Lebrun.

> As examples in art of complete womanliness, mention may be made of two exquisite portraits by Madame Lebrun, in which whilst representing her little daughter and

herself, the painter discloses the inner essence and the life of maternal love, and discloses them with a caressing playfulness of passion unattainable by men, and sometimes unappreciated by men. Here, indeed, we have the poetry of universal motherhood, common to the household hearts of good women the wide world over.[62]

Other critics have pointed out that Mary Cassatt often chose the subject of women and children, that Käthe Kollwitz showed a very womanly concern for the exploited, that Rosalba Carriera used the feminine medium of pastel, and that women have excelled in the more "passive" medium of photography.

While all these points are no doubt well taken, it must be said that men, too, have often portrayed motherhood, which, after all, is a universal theme; that human compassion is certainly not a monopoly of women; that pastel was used by male artists long before Carriera, and that photography was not the invention of women but had been used with magnificent results by male photographers years before Julia Cameron was given a camera by her daughter. And even if this distinction between characteristically masculine and feminine qualities in art is valid, it is obvious that they are not necessarily the result of the sex of the artist, since there are very masculine women artists like Artemisia Gentileschi or Rosa Bonheur, and there are very delicate and even feminine male artists such as Fragonard or Redon. The truth is that these sex roles are probably more determined by the values and ideals of society than by the nature of the two sexes. As John Stuart Mill said more than a hundred years ago in *The Subjection of Women,*

> Neither does it avail anything to say that the nature of the two sexes adapts them to their present functions and position, and renders these appropriate to them. Standing on the ground of common sense and the constitution of the human mind, I deny that any one knows, or can know, the nature of the two sexes, as long as they have only been seen in their present relation to one another. If men had ever been found in society without women, or women without men, or if there had been a society of men and women in which the women were not under control of the men, something might have been positively known about the mental and moral differences which may be inherent in the nature of each. What is now called the nature of women is an eminently artificial thing—the result of forced repression in some directions, unnatural stimulation in others.[63]

Obviously, it is useless to speculate on what women would be like if they were totally divorced from men. Since we are dealing with art rather than psychology, it seems more important to try to determine what the social and cultural circumstances have been that gave rise to women artists, and which conditions have been detrimental to their development. Clearly the view held by Mill (and implied by most feminists) that women were suppressed in early times and are becoming more outstanding as artists as more opportunities are open to them is a misrepresentation of the facts. Actually women artists were probably most important in Neolithic times in contrast to the earlier Paleolithic period when they were apparently completely absorbed in domestic activities, a state of affairs still existing in some primitive societies. It would seem that their cultural role was sharply curtailed in the ancient worlds starting with the establishment of the great historical civilizations of Mesopotamia and Egypt and

[62]Sparrow, *Women Painters,* p. 11.
[63]John Stuart Mill, *The Subjection of Women* (London, 1869), p. 38.

continuing in classical times under the Greeks and Romans. This development was undoubtedly the result of changing social conditions, proving conclusively that social forces can have an overwhelming influence on the contribution of an entire sex or social class to the culture of a period. It can also be demonstrated that the position of women in art as both patrons and practitioners began to improve slowly during the Middle Ages, although largely restricted to crafts; that women played a modest role in the so-called fine arts during the Renaissance, a role that increased during the Baroque and Rococo periods; and finally, about two hundred years ago, they began to play an important part in the cultural life first of Europe and then of America. Yet, this development has by no means been a steady advance, for, interestingly enough, women were more prominent in the art of the ancient regime of the late eighteenth century than after the French Revolution. In literature, they were more important in the early part of the nineteenth century than in the later part, and, with the exception of sculpture and photography, they have not played as great a role in the visual arts of the twentieth century as they did in the second half of the nineteenth. The answer must be that, though social conditions govern the opportunities open to women artists, creativity itself springs from deeper, more mysterious sources. Greatness is not just the result of favorable circumstances. If it were, it would be difficult to account for artists like Van Gogh and Dostoevski, who proved themselves against all odds, for it was indeed in their stars and not in their sex, education, or position that their destiny lay.

INDEX

Boldface numbers refer to illustrations.